WEEDING OUT
THE TARGET
POPULATION

Recent Titles in Contributions in Sociology
Series Editor: Don Martindale

WEEDING OUT
THE TARGET
POPULATION

The Law of Accountability
in a
Manpower Program

JAMES LATIMORE

Contributions in Sociology, Number 54

Greenwood Press
Westport, Connecticut · London, England

Library of Congress Cataloging in Publication Data

Latimore, James.
  Weeding out the target population.

  (Contributions in sociology, ISSN 0084-9278 ; no. 54)
  Bibliography: p.
  Includes index.
  1. Youth Employment Agency (U.S.)   2. Manpower policy
—United States.   3. Youth—Employment—United States.
I. Title. II. Series.
HD6273.L38   1985   331.3'412042'0973   84-8952
ISBN 0-313-24495-2 (lib. bdg.)

Library of Congress Catalog Card Number: 84-8952
ISBN: 0-313-24495-2
ISSN: 0084-9278

First published in 1985

Greenwood Press
A division of Congressional Information Service, Inc.
88 Post Road West
Westport, Connecticut 06881

Printed in the United States of America

10 9 8 7 6 5 4 3 2 1

Contents

Figures and Tables

Preface

Philanthropy is not very highly regarded by social planners, and it is indeed deplorable for all the reasons frequently advanced. But philanthropy is not so bad—I would even say it is good—insofar as it reflects a concern for those to be helped. The welfare state is good when it alleviates the conditions philanthropy is focused on. Then again, it is bad when it weakens the sense of concern, when it pits one interest group against another for a share of the spoils.

One of the most troublesome dilemmas faced by any society is how to motivate people to contribute to production without totally abandoning to their own fate those who fail to do so. Private philanthropy, the welfare state, socialism, communism, communalism—all represent attempts to deal with this in different ways. Some lean toward the motivational end, using material incentives and minimizing "protection." Others lean toward "protection," and then motivation becomes more of a problem, especially when material incentives are de-emphasized.

The overlap of philanthropy and welfare state in a particular historical period gives rise to its own problems. The subsidy of philanthropy through tax law, in the form of allowable deductions for contributions, does not seem to raise the issue of control and accountability. However, when there is a direct transfer of public funds to philanthropic organizations it is a different matter—even when, on the surface, there is a common purpose.

The structure of organizations—political and otherwise—as well as their relations with each other can probably be most economically expressed in terms of accountability. Who is accountable to whom? In what terms? And what is the cost of non-compliance or failure? The importance of accountability in a democratic-rational legal system can be acknowledged, while at the same time noting the problems that arise when government bureaucracies impose their own internal accounting on the outside world. The Youth Employment Agency (YEA), as it will be called here, was selected for study (1) because it was in the process of transition from a financially independent philanthropic organization devoted to job counseling and job placement for youths with correctional records to one increasingly dependent on federal grants and (2) because the opportunity existed to observe the organization over a period of several years.

Small organizations like YEA become "bureaucratic" not so much directly as by affiliation with larger, much more bureaucratized ones. This is the process of bureaucratization seen in this study. YEA itself became somewhat more bureaucratic, with a greater degree of specialization and more written memos and formal rules. But far more important was its "bureaucratization by affiliation," in which it became a branch office of a federal bureaucracy, that is, the U.S. Department of Labor and its Comprehensive Employment and Training Act (CETA) program.

The unemployed as a whole can be categorized, reduced to statistics and "parameters," but particular organizations such as YEA are dealing with particular individuals who at a given time are likely to be "atypical" or somewhat unique, requiring labor-intensive effort rather than prepackaged solutions dictated by funding and accountability requirements. The aim, which should be *good results* (an aim on which all agree) turns out perversely to be *good reports* in the statistical sense. The strengths of philanthropic intervention—commitment to a mission, a deep concern for clients, organizational solidarity, flexibility, and so on—may be negated by certain practices such as those encompassed by the term *bureaucratic accountability*.

As this is written, a new manpower program is taking shape, based on greater decentralization and "debureaucratization." However, if authorization and appropriation are accomplished in Washington, centralized decision-making and uniform standards are probably not far behind. The alternatives, including programs funded and administered by the states, entail obvious inequities and represent the other horn of a dilemma. Certain programs can probably be effectively centralized: voting rights, for example. Others, such as manpower programs, can easily be overcentralized given local conditions, changing conditions over time, and less-than-adequate knowledge of all the forces at work. It requires some wisdom (and courage) to recognize the difference. The central question should be what is happening to *people* at the bottom, rather than how is the *program* doing. The problems are formidable and any solutions may of necessity be particular and temporary. However, a study focused on this problem alone is necessary to do it justice. The present study is therefore essentially limited to describing organizational life at the bottom of the pyramid of accountability.

WEEDING OUT
THE TARGET
POPULATION

1

The Agency and Its Clients

Philanthropic organizations in America play an important part in resolving a conflict between the functions of government related to the general welfare of the population and a political philosophy that discourages if not forbids direct intervention by government in many areas. Leaving aside the task of maintaining public safety (in which there is government intervention), four of the most important sectors of life, both in sustaining it and in enhancing its quality, are health, work, the arts, and the quality of the community. In all these government can take only a tentative, often indirect, part. Societal needs and political philosophy are, in fact, bound together in a doctrine of freedom: You are free to help whomever you wish to help or to aid whatever cause you think worthy of aid. Tax laws and slogans encourage but don't require us to "do our share."

Philanthropy is a sizable industry in the United States. Large sums of money are contributed each year. The United Way campaign alone raised $1.8 billion in 1981, while the contributions to all philanthropic organizations totaled $53.6 billion that year.[1] There were, in 1979, nearly 28,000 non-governmental non-profit organizations whose goal was "to maintain or aid social, educational, religious, or other activities deemed to serve the common good." They ranged in size from a handful of workers to nation-wide giants like the Red Cross with a large staff and over 1 million volunteers. About half had assets of less than $100,000, however.

The wide variety of services provided or supported by these organizations often reflects the many ills and misfortunes that can befall us, either by filling the gap between need and the aid supplied by government or by first identifying the need, as in such cases as natural disasters, disease, old age, unwanted pregnancy, poverty, alcoholism, learning disability, illiteracy, physical abuse of children or spouses, unemployment, or simply a Christmas without toys. Some services, on the other hand, contribute directly to the intellectual and artistic quality of life, for example, subsidies for the arts, foreign exchange programs, research and demonstration grants.

The Youth Employment Agency (YEA) is one of these 28,000 philanthropic organizations. As the name implies, it deals with the problem of employment for youth, in this case urban youth and, more specifically, those with severe employment handicaps.

YEA was 40 years old in 1976. Granted a charter by the state in 1936 as a private, not-for-profit corporation, its purpose was "to provide vocational guidance and job placement for 16–21 year-old probationers and parolees from correctional institutions and training schools."[2] The middle of the Depression was not the most favorable time to launch an employment service, especially for such a clientele. The organization is "classified by the Internal Revenue Service as a 'public supported charity' . . . not a money-granting foundation, although it has such powers in its charter."[3]

The principal founder (now chairman of the agency's board of directors) is of colonial stock. His first paternal American ancestor came to this country from England in 1630 and settled in Braintree, Massachusetts.[4]

When the agency was chartered, the founder was fresh out of Yale Law School. His father, a physician, was at one time commissioner of corrections for the state.[5] The father's interest in penology appears to have been carried on by the son, with the difference that the latter has involved himself in both the philanthropic and the "official" aspects of the problem: In 1935–36, he was a special assistant attorney general for the state.

The founder's career is described in Who's Who in America. In the late thirties he was an associate in a Center City law firm; then he became an assistant U.S. attorney. During World War II he worked in Washington, ending up in 1945 as general counsel for the Foreign Economic Administration. He returned to Center City after the war as a senior partner in a law firm. In the mid-fifties he left the practice of law. Since that time his career was in business and investment. He was president of a major Center City newspaper.[6] Since 1960 he was president of a company that owns television and radio stations and various periodicals. The chairman also was involved in Republican party affairs, principally as a fund-raiser. However, he was selected for two presidential commissions, one having to do with campaign costs and the other dealing with reorganization of the executive department.

Without the founder's wealth and influence, there would probably be no Youth Employment Agency. He is the benefactor of the organization as well as of the organization's troubled clients. This is not to say that the agency has been totally dependent on him for every dollar it gets. In recent years, it has been fairly successful in obtaining government funds on its own initiative. At the same time, the political contacts of the founder have not always yielded contracts or grants. Without him, however, the agency probably would have been disbanded long ago. Even today, the amount of money he personally can raise each year is sufficient to keep the agency running, though on a much smaller scale.

The early days of the agency can be partially glimpsed in the records of meetings. The minutes of the board meeting of January 14, 1942, for example, show that the staff reported the "No. of Boys Handled" during the month of December 1941 was 103, about half the intake in recent times. The complete activities for the month are shown in Table 1.1.

The expenses reported in the meeting indicate that the agency's annual budget was about $24,000 and that it had a staff of six people. The 1976 budget was approximately $1 million, including salaries for 42 people. For those interested in the details the complete financial report, showing income and expenses for December 1941, is provided in Table 1.2.

Table 1.1
Number of Boys Handled and Jobs Obtained during Month of December 1941

No. of Boys : Handled :	SOURCE OF REFERRAL	: No. of Jobs : Obtained
W : N : TOT:		: W : N : Total
26 :40 : 66 :	State Training Schools	:17 :23 : 40
2 : 0 : 2 :	State Vocational Info Program	: 3 : 0 : 3
3 : 0 : 3 :	Parole	: 1 : 0 : 1
9 : 3 : 12 :	Probation	: 4 : 2 : 6
2 : 0 : 2 :	U.S. District Court	: 1 : 0 : 1
3 : 3 : 6 :	Youth Bureau	: 1 : 2 : 3
8 : 4 : 12 :	Miscellaneous	: 2 : 3 : 5
53 :50 :103 :		:29 :30 : 59

	W : N : Total
No. of cases active previous month	28 :31 : 59
" " " newly registered current mo.	11 :10 : 21
" " " re-registered	14 : 9 : 23

No. of Office Interviews	257
Employer Contacts	260
Appts. Arranged for Boys	130
Miscellaneous Contacts	135

NOTE: W = White; N = Negro.

Table 1.2
Financial Report, January 12, 1942

DECEMBER

Balance on hand	$2717.84
Donations - 39 contributors	2104.50
Income - Annual Dinner	183.50
Income - Tickets, Amer. Football Charity	12.35
Loans repaid	6.60
	$5024.79

Disbursements:

Director's salary	261.52
Assistant Directors' salaries	583.33
Office staff salaries	360.00
Rent	100.00
Electricity	8.84
Tel. & Tel.	100.29
Stationery & Stamps	174.29
Office equipment	60.90
Loans to boys	42.35
Carfares	12.65
Lunches & Dinners	17.85
Printer's bills	203.10
Expenses - Annual Dinner	370.59
Publicity	10.00
Overtime	25.00
Miscellaneous	433.79
	$2764.50

ON HAND: January 1st, 1942	$2260.29	
Receipts, January	152.90	
	$2413.19	
Disbursements, January		855.53
ON HAND: January 12, 1942	$1557.66	

In one important way the concerns of the board at the 1942 meeting were different. There was considerable discussion about the role of the agency in the war effort.

The staff of [YEA] held a meeting to discuss the participation or role that the organization could play in the Defense Program. It was decided that the [YEA] could be most useful in any plans that would be devised to develop Civilian Defense activities within training schools, recognizing that youth morale was a basic responsibility both inside and outside the institution of social workers whose program rested largely around the rehabilitation of juvenile delinquents . . . .

But in other ways the organization seems the same, especially in a most important way: money problems and fund-raising. It was reported at the meeting that the Christmas fund-raising campaign "showed improvement but did not come up to our expectations." In 1939, $797.50 had been raised from 83 contributors; in 1940 the amount raised was $1,383 (from 60 contributors); and in 1941 the fund-raising effort brought in $1,914.50 (from 83 contributors). However, finances were still, in the words of one member, "a serious and urgent matter." There was no doubt that "the war situation will seriously affect the income of the agency," she observed, even though the war had "no effect on the intake of boys." The need was "as great if not greater than ever, for the services of YEA," she added.

It was decided to seek state funds. One board member suggested that the legislature might add funds for job placements to the budget of the state training school, whose clients were often sent to YEA. Three members, including the founder, were asked to "present the issue to the Governor." The board also worked out a plan for contacting certain wealthy individuals and certain foundations. Finally, it was noted in the minutes that the founder "pledged to raise five thousand dollars within the next thirty days"—a substantial sum of money at that time, and about 20 percent of the agency's annual budget.

In the post-war period, females were added to the agency's clientele. The employment report for 1947 (Table 1.3) shows that 22.5 percent of the clients that year were females.

Although most clients were placed in unskilled jobs, especially messenger and delivery jobs, a surprisingly large number were placed in

Table 1.3
Employment Report, January 1–December 31, 1947

New Registration				Re-Registration				Placements			
Negro		White		Negro		White		Negro		White	
Boys	Girls	Boys	Girls	Boys	Girls	Boys	Girls	Boys	Girls	Boys	Girls
193	59	243	85	173	25	106	39	224	46	195	74
252		328		198		145		270		269	

Total Number of Applicants   923
Total Number of Placements   539

semi-skilled, skilled, or clerical jobs. In the first three months of 1947, for example, the agency reported 141 placements, of which 34 were classified as skilled or semi-skilled and 13 were clerical jobs. These three categories represented about a third of all placements. The occupational classification of the placements for that period, and the breakdown by sex, is shown in Table 1.4; it gives the reader some idea of the particular jobs involved.

The economy of the city at the time is reflected in the industrial classification of the jobs in which clients were placed. Manufacturing accounted for the largest share of placements: 53 percent of the placements in this period were in a variety of manufacturing firms, textiles and printing particularly. Firms in the service industry, including restaurants, messenger services, hospitals, and auto services, provided 53 jobs (37 percent). Retail establishments absorbed only 6 percent of the placed clients during this period. These included florist shops, whose need for delivery boys would increase dramatically during certain holiday periods. Finally, the insurance and financial industries accounted for only 4 percent of the placements.

We can view the agency's performance during this period in another way. In the agency files was a detailed report covering the clients seen from February 1 through August 21, 1947. The report lists the clients' names and addresses, the date on which each was registered at YEA, the agency that referred the client to YEA, the date on which each was

Table 1.4
Occupational Distribution of Placements, January–March 1947

MAJOR OCCUPATIONAL CLASSIFICATIONS	MALE	FEMALE
Clerical Workers (office boy, filing, etc.)	5	8
Personal and Building Service (waitress, elevator operator, busgirl, bellhop, kitchen helper, porter, etc.)	9	9
Skilled Craftsmen (baker, silkscreening, leather repairs	6	4
Semi-skilled Production Workers (floorgirl, assembling, sewing, machine operating, printing, darkroom)	16	8
Unskilled (packing, shipping, general assistant, fill bottles, delivery, and laundry shaker)	44	4
Messenger	28	0

placed in a job (if he or she was), the employer's name and address, the job title, and the client's wage or salary. There were 204 clients seen during that period. Of these, 97 were placed on at least one job (a placement rate of 48 percent), and 56 of them (57 percent) were placed within three days after registration—with most of these being placed on the same day or the next day. Given the clientele, this performance seems remarkable, even if many of the jobs did require little skill.

In the early fifties the agency was involved in a war of a different kind: youth gangs. This stage of the agency's history was described some years later in a national Sunday-supplement magazine. One of YEA's "more spectacular achievements" was the part it played in "breaking up the city's notorious fighting street gangs," the article said.[7] YEA's part in the city's effort to control the gangs was focused on finding jobs for gang members. The director of the agency at that time recalled: "What we did was to persuade some of the leaders to come to us. We got them good jobs. When the rank-and-file fighters saw what their leaders were doing, they swarmed in here, too. And before you knew it, there were no more fighting street gangs." From this came the agency's first contract with the city for the provision of employment-related services to youth and, quite suddenly, a reputation as an effective agency that extended beyond the relatively small world of probation and parole workers upon whom it had depended before. It was a turning point for YEA.

A "Historical Perspective" printed by the agency in 1977 notes that by 1964 "YEA had come to be regarded by the courts and youth serving agencies as the last resort for their hardest-to-place and most difficult youths. The State wished to establish a priority with YEA for the young people under its jurisdiction and thus entered into a contract for services through the Department of Social Welfare and the Home Service Bureau."

In 1967, "training was added to the YEA program through an On-the-Job Training prime contract with the U.S. Department of Labor. . . ." Out of this experience the agency, "in cooperation with the professional design societies" of the city, developed a program for training "school dropouts and ex-addicts as engineering and architectural draftsmen and steel detailers . . . . Since 1970, over 200 junior draftsmen have been trained and employed." The program was being replicated in another large city not too far away. The program was publicized in several articles in the city's newspapers. An article in one paper (undated, circa 1971) began by describing the case of a trainee in the program who at age 16 had dropped out of school and had since held "several odd jobs—including a short stint in the Navy." Now, the author added, the young man was "one of 22 youngsters beginning a job training plan combined with classroom studies sponsored by a coalition of engineers and architects in cooperation with the Youth Employment Agency." The trainees would "study half-days in YEA class-rooms, and then spend afternoons in the offices of cooperating firms" for on-the-job training and work assignments. "After six months, they will enter the companies on a full-time basis, continuing their training for another five months." Recruits for the program, the article pointed out, were "screened from nearly 3000 youths visiting the non-profit YEA each year."

Nineteen seventy-three brought "a pilot project funded by the city's Addiction Services Agency" designed to serve "up to 500 ex-addicts." The project included a "skills training component" in which the services of established commercial and non-profit training facilities could be paid for, avoiding the expense of setting up a new training program. The following year another pilot project was established, "under the auspices of the city's Criminal Justice Coordinating Council, to serve youth in the criminal justice system." This program included subcontracted skills training also, as well as "remedial education services and high school equivalency preparation."

The document concluded:

Over the years, YEA has had contractual relationships on the City, State, and Federal levels. Locally, as many as 298 social service agencies have used the agency's services in a single year . . . . Since 1967, YEA has worked with 21,250 different youths. The staff has developed 57,633 jobs for these youth and 19,185 placements have been effected.

Despite the increasing amount of government funding, however, the document noted that there was "a continuing need for unrestricted and private monies" to manage programs and to undertake new initiatives. Without such funds "YEA would have to respond to the politics of the day rather than to the needs of youth," a theme that recurs frequently in the agency's publications.

DAILY OPERATIONS

In 1973 YEA was located in an aging office building on Center City's "social work row," a street so named because of the numerous social-welfare agencies located there. The space was broken up into many cubicles or offices. Only the director had a truly private office with floor-to-ceiling walls. The other offices were open at the top; plasterboard walls extended about seven feet from the floor, with a folding vinyl door that could be closed for visual privacy.

The workday at the agency began at 8:30 A.M. Usually there were four or five clients waiting downstairs in the lobby when the first workers arrived. When the office opened, clients got off the elevator and entered the waiting room. It was the largest room of all and contained the registration desk and seating space for about 30 people. The seats were molded fiberglass chairs, and there was one sofa. All the furnishings except the registration desk were donated by corporations redecorating their own offices. For the corporations, the donated furniture qualified as charitable contributions for tax purposes. This made it possible for YEA to obtain furnishings at no cost—used, but clean and useful. The registration desk resembled a not-quite-chest-high bank counter, with a dark formica top and stained plywood below.

The kids—they range in age from 16 to 21—come to YEA on referral from such sources as courts, schools, probation officers, churches, and correctional institutions. The line usually forms early each morning outside YEA's . . . office, with each youngster praying that behind that door lies the key to straightening out his troubled life.[8]

All clients were required to check in at the registration desk upon arrival. New clients had to be checked off against the "appointment book," a large ledger with the names of clients scheduled for intake that day. Appointments for these clients had been made in advance by their "referral workers"—counselors and social workers at the numerous other agencies who sent their clients to YEA when job placement was desired. Some of these clients were referred on the basis of contracts, which provided YEA with a big part of its income. Others were "non-contract referrals." The appointment book also contained the name of the referral agency and the referral worker, the client's age and address, and time of appointment. The client was sent a postcard a few days before the scheduled appointment as a reminder.

Jim Smith, a 17-year-old high school dropout, had almost nothing going for him. His broken home had seen no father for more than ten years. The family was on relief. An older brother was in prison for armed robbery. Jim had a police record for purse-snatching. He could read simple comic books but not much more.

"Old" clients had to check in also, but merely for the purpose of signing their names to the "sign-in book," another large ledger volume that all clients signed to verify (for the agency) that they were there. The clerks on the registration desk then pulled the client's folder and placed it on a table at the bottom of the stack of folders. The client then sat down and waited. Magazines, some second-hand brought in by staff members, others sent on free subscriptions by a few publishing companies that could be persuaded to contribute in this fashion, were available for passing the time. Sometimes the clients knew each other and would talk; mostly they did not. They would leaf through the magazines or look out the window, or occasionally listen to their radios. The director would pass through the waiting room when he came in, and if any clients had their caps or hats on, he would say as he strode through, "Gentlemen, please remove your hats!"

The counselors would come out to the table where the client folders were piled when they had finished with one case, take the top folder, and call out the client's name. The client would then go into the counselor's office.

After a while, if it was a busy morning, clients were shifting in their seats, the magazines tossed aside and hunger setting in. Clients who had been seen by a counselor might be queried by others on the way out: "What did you get?" If a client had an appointment card for a job interview, it was good news and seemed to make the others' wait worthwhile. If, on the other hand, a client left with "nothin," the information would be greeted by a chorus of soft curses.

Jim Smith kept his appointment at YEA, though he hated to parade himself as a failure. He was soon in private session with a sympathetic counselor . . . . The day after his preliminary interview, Jim had a temporary job as a hospital porter at $77 a week. Subsequent interviews disclosed that he was adept with his hands and had an attraction to machinery. He's now in a printing plant earning $100 a week.

By the end of the morning the last client would have been seen, the waiting room emptied, the ash trays full—and the counselors would take a breather, chatting about unusual or problem cases. There appeared to be a certain satisfaction gained from clearing out the waiting room. Lunchtime was ahead. The afternoon might be spent in seeing one or two applicants for part-time jobs, some follow-up phone calls (checking to see if a client was hired, for example), and "paperwork." Paperwork included filling in the daily sheets and making entries in the clients' folders. The daily sheets were large, oversized pages containing the names of the clients seen that day, their age, and the referring agency. When these were typed up by the clerk after the morning rush, the counselors had to record on the sheets where the clients were referred for a job, if they were. When clients were hired and the hire was verified by a phone call, the counselor had to look up the daily sheet for the day of referral and enter the "disposition." The same procedure was necessary if the client was not hired.

The swift and humane manner in which YEA salvaged the bleak life of Jim Smith seems extraordinary, especially in that it didn't cost either Jim or the employer a cent. YEA is supported almost entirely by private contributions and has reduced red tape to a minimum. It places nearly 3000 Jim Smiths annually into "instant jobs" and is currently attempting an expansion to reach more of them in slum areas.

Around four o'clock, the necessary work for the day was usually finished. The hour from four to five was relaxed. One counselor might drop by the office of another for "consultation" and remain for some time. Another one or two (male) would stop by the registration desk to check appointments for the next day, then remain for 15 to 20 minutes talking with the female clerks. At 4:30, those who were on "early hours" (and who opened up in the mornings at 8:30) would go home. At five, the others followed. The director and one or two administrators might remain behind, sometimes working, but more often talking—about personal matters if the day was good or agency problems if not. When they left, the elevator door was locked so no one could get off on that floor.

In 1974 the agency moved two blocks down the street to larger quarters. A new contract (the addict program), which required hiring 14 new staff members, had been signed: new money, new resources (video-tape machines, remedial education, skills training), new challenges—and brand new offices. The new office was also in an older building. The agency was able to get a larger amount of space with customized renovations at a rate that fit within its new budget, but only by signing a ten-year lease for $55,000 per year. The duration of the lease and the annual rent represented substantial new obligations. After the renovations and the painting and decorations, the office looked quite impressive and pleasant, with abstract lithographs and posters loaned by the chairman on the walls. In the new waiting room were close-up photographic portraits of clients. The director had the corner office as before. This time, however, it was far away from the waiting room and the counselors.

After the move, waiting time for clients in the new quarters was substantially reduced. Counselors had complained about the time clients had to spend in the waiting room, and discussed the merits of seeing all clients, even old ones, by appointment only. That would eliminate the waiting time. The new policy was instituted shortly after moving into the new offices. This was more efficient, though some of the vitality, confusion, urgency, and liveliness of the old way was lacking.

With the addition of new specialists, the clients were passed on to the counselors only after they had been through an "orientation program" and, in most cases, a "job-preparation workshop." The purpose of orientation was to acquaint clients with the functions and procedures of the agency. The job-preparation workshop was to prepare them for job interviews through lectures, discussions, and videotaped client performances in a mock-interview situation. If the counselor succeeded in placing the client on a job, the client was then transferred to another new specialist—the post-placement counselor (PPC), or job monitor. The PPC was supposed to help the client adjust to a new job in whatever way possible. This sometimes involved negotiating with the employer on behalf of the client, explaining absences from work, and so on. But for the most part the PPCs concentrated on getting the client to understand and accept the obligations of the job so that crises would not occur.

The young people helped by YEA are usually grateful beyond their ability to express. They mumble their thanks with a sincerity that runs deep. Others in the picture are more vocal. Says a reform school superintendent: "I don't know how we could help our boys if we had no YEA." And a settlement house director: "I can't thank YEA enough for the way it handled some of my difficult cases." And the personnel manager of a large retail chain: "YEA has been of tremendous help in screening applicants for our beginner jobs. My life has been made easy."

STRUCTURE OF THE AGENCY

In 1973 the staff of the agency consisted of 24 full-time and two part-time workers. The full-time staff included an executive director, an associate director, an office administrator, a program director, a director of the on-the-job training (OJT) project, a supervisor of counselors, six counselors, one administrative assistant, two bookkeepers, three clerks, and an information center director. The staff of the agency was organized as shown in Figure 1.1. The solid lines between boxes represent the formal authority—responsibility relationships—while the dotted lines represent a relationship to the associate director for certain specific functions. For example, the office administrator was responsible to the associate director for "administration," on matters related to clerical staffing and performance, intake procedures, and so on. The office administrator was responsible to the director for "fiscal" affairs. The job description, on this point, lists the following: "Oversees fiscal administration and liaison with contract agencies, including voucher preparation. Does payroll, accounts payable and bookkeeping with the assistance of the accounting firm."

The OJT project director had divided responsibility also. She was responsible to the director for overall management (including results) of the project, and to the associate director "for daily operations and coordination with general program."

The program developer was responsible only to the director, but in

Figure 1.1
YEA Staff Organization, 1973

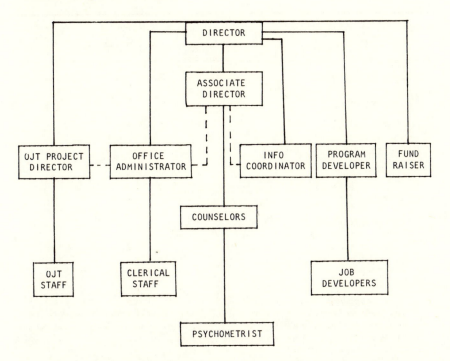

practice the added responsibility of supervising job development required working with the associate director.

These five people made up the "executive staff" of the agency. The internal and external relations of the executive staff as a whole more accurately depicts the authority-responsibility relationships than does the "official" chart. In the executive staff, the associate director was equal with rather than superior to other members of the group. Others on the executive staff frequently coordinated with the associate director but cannot be said to have reported to him officially. On any important matters when conflict existed, members of the executive staff could take it up with the director or with the group as a whole.

When the second phase of this study commenced, after relocation to the new offices, there were 46 people on the staff. The agency's "organizational chart" and "client flow chart" are reproduced in Appendixes A and B. The principal changes in staffing compared with 1973 are shown in Table 1.5. One functional position, that of program director, was eliminated. The position was combined with supervision of job developers. The latter position still exists. Thus, the change in the su-

Table 1.5
Changes in Staffing, 1973–1976

Position	1973 Staff (N=24)	1976 Staff (N=46)	CHANGES (1976)
Administrators	3	3	Same
Supervisors	3	4	+1
Admin. Assts.	1	3	+2
Counselors	6	11	+5
PPCs *	0	6	+6
Clerks	6	10	+4
Job Developers	3	4	+1
Remedial Educ.	0	2	+2
Bookkeepers	2	3	+1

*Post-placement counselors, sometimes referred to as post-placement monitors or assistant counselors. Their responsibilities were to monitor clients' progress on the job, deal with problems that might arise, locate clients who left a job, and so on. They usually were minority-group members.

pervisor category is the addition of the addict-program supervisor. In 1976 the executive staff was composed of all administrators and supervisors. However, there was an inner elite composed of the "old hands"— the executive director, associate director, fiscal administrator, and OJT director—which met informally and made up the *real* executive staff.

In general, the increase in size and program mix was accompanied by greater specialization, a more formal mode of operations, and the creation of new "assistant" positions, even though in at least one respect the agency became less bureaucratic with expansion. The number of support personnel (administrators, supervisors, administrative assistants, bookkeepers, and clerks) remained virtually the same, while the total size increased. The ratio of administrators and supervisors to total staff was 1 to 4 in 1973 and 1 to 6 in 1976. Only one supervisor was added, while the staff as a whole increased by 18. In part, this may have been made easier for the administrators and supervisors by the increase in administrative assistants. The ratio of administrative assistants to administrators and supervisors in 1973 was 1 to 6, while in 1976 it was 1 to 2. In other words, there were more administrative assistants per administrator or supervisor. However, much of this added capacity appears to have been devoted to accountability tasks (records and statistics and reports). This should have enabled the administrators and supervisors to spend more time on supervising the actual work of the agency and meeting with counselors, but this does not seem to have occurred. One reason may be that the requirements of accountability increased faster than the staff allocated for that purpose. The associate director had *his* administrative assistant prepare a list of the kinds of data the agency had to gather and the reports it had to make (see Appendix C). The assistant spent full time on such tasks. The associate director also spent more time than ever on statistics and was less able to keep up with the task. He delegated all of his direct involvement in the work of the counselors to other supervisors; whereas before he had regulated the flow of the work load, assigning special cases to certain counselors, checking to see how many clients showed up, who was placed where, how many placements were made by whom, and in general policing the work of the counselors, now he had no direct contact with counselors and seldom ventured beyond his immediate area. He claimed that this was more efficient. "We've got a *system* now. The Counseling Supervisor [decides] which ones go to OJT, which ones go to her staff. She assigns the kids from Orientation into certain counselors." He continued:

She's better at it than I am because she's immersed in it. The only time I go out there is to look at level of intake in a general way, see how many kids have come in that day; just to have some sort of tuning in. Now, it's more efficient, in terms of allocation of kids to counselors, than ever before.

Earlier, the director could personally observe what staff members were doing. The office was smaller and his own office was in the line of traffic. Problems that came up were often settled in "corridor conferences." Informal communication between members of various departments was the norm. There was a minimum of memo-writing and those that were written were often done for the purpose of making official what had been decided informally.

The expansion of the agency, however, led in the direction of more specialization. New specialized positions included post-placement counselors and remedial education teachers. The supervisor of the addict program also arranged for skills training at outside facilities. These represent new technologies rather than a division of the old work into more specialties.

The time clock was a symbol of the more impersonal relations in the agency. It was added shortly after the staff moved into the new offices. All personnel were required to punch in and out. When the associate director was asked if the time clock had made any difference in punctuality or if anyone had been docked for lateness, he replied that, overall, it had made some difference. It had provided "a definite record as a basis for discussing lateness" with the staff, and a record of man hours spent on the various contracts. As for docking: "G__ (Director), to his credit, explained to the staff initially that the clock was not for punitive purposes. No one has been docked or laid off as a result of the clock. The staff accepted this after some initial misgivings."

Whether the clock was used punitively or not, it was a symbol of more impersonal relationships—a new phenomenon in the agency. Whatever the explanation—whether increased delegation and distance, increased specialization, or increased accountability—the agency appeared to be both more formal and more fragmented into separate programs in 1976 compared with the earlier period. Despite his faith in the new "system," the associate director was aware of some of the problems and dilemmas associated with the transition. When asked how his job had changed in recent years, he replied: "I have had to use all my skills to avoid frustration. By delegation—required in a larger organization. But I still get involved in all sorts of problems . . . . "

Part of the problem with the formal structure was that the associate director could not divorce himself from routine matters. However, he did not want the organization to become a "rote-ish agency" either, with a highly specialized division of labor and impersonal relationships. There were problems either way, as he noted:

I don't want to get the feeling that this agency is becoming a rote-ish agency, in that this is my job and not somebody else's job; you can have a whole other kind of contamination. But delegation—good delegation, not just passing the buck—is so important. If you start playing with all kinds of things, you're going to dilute yourself.

A description of the agency's structure (and its conflicts) is not complete without mention of its board of directors and its chairman. The policies of YEA, and any operational procedure that affected the agency's mission, were decided by the board. In reality, these decisions were often made by the chairman.

A few board members were simply family friends or personal friends of the chairman and thus had a special and unique interest. Most others, excluding the former director and the two "professionals" on the board, had an interest in good relations with the chairman—an interest of an economic nature, though not necessarily direct and immediate. Several either worked for him or worked for a company or foundation owned by the individual who controlled the corporation that the chairman headed. The chairman, in other words, "worked for" a man even wealthier than he (but one who took no particular interest in YEA except to make financial contributions).

The executive director outlined, during the course of an interview, various affiliations between the chairman and his current associates on the board. The chairman (and founder) was, as previously noted, chairman of the board of a corporation owning television stations, radio stations, and various periodicals (one a Sunday-newspaper magazine distributed nationally). In addition, he was a partner in an investment firm. Both of these firms were owned by one man, a member of a wealthy and distinguished Center City family. The president of YEA at the time was also president of a foundation that bore the name of the same man. YEA's president was a protégé of the chairman and a former subordinate. The vice president was a partner in the investment firm. The vice chairman of YEA (an honorary title for a former president) was a former law partner of the chairman. The treasurer was a partner in the investment firm. The secretary worked for a related company. These people made up the executive committee—the group most knowledgeable about the agency's work, most active in the formation of policy, and most closely attached to the chairman through business relationships.

Thus, of the 25 members of the Board, 14 were either employees, friends, relatives, or business associates of the chairman; four were friends or associates of other directors but not the chairman; and three were friends and associates of the executive director. The executive director himself and a former executive director are also members of the board, as are two former clients. It was clear that the chairman of YEA exercised considerable control over the agency through his relationships with the key board members; his decisions and ideas were communicated through them (and sometimes directly) to the executive director.

THE AGENCY'S SELF-PORTRAIT

Organizations manage the impressions they project to other organizations and individuals; the picture that an organization presents also defines some of its goals, and what it considers to be successful performance. The self-portrait is related to the agency's "mission"; its purpose is to sell the agency and its mission to prospective contributors, contractors, and supporters.

In its literature and reports directed to funding agencies and contributors, the agency referred to its clients as "the hardest to place youngsters" in the city. Other elements of the self-portrait are:

Efficiency, due to its private (as opposed to public) nature. This includes instant action, no red tape, flexibility, and a businesslike approach.

Low cost, due to its resulting efficiency.

Leadership, showing the way for other agencies, especially public agencies. This again is alleged to be due to the fact that it was a private agency, free of the restraints and red tape typical of government bureaucracy.

Personal attention to each client, due to the agency's small size and indirectly due to the fact that, unlike public agencies burdened with bureaucrats, counselors who do not perform satisfactorily in serving clients' needs could easily be fired. Thus, the staff was presented as hard-working and dedicated. Personal attention also entails continuing availability of service: YEA never gave up on a client.

The self-portrait was based upon the function of job placement. All the qualities that facilitated placement, together with the hard-to-place clientele, helped to substantiate the agency's claim to *uniqueness*, an important aspect of the agency's mission, which is discussed later.

The chairman's annual fund-raising letter was sent to wealthy friends and business acquaintances shortly before Christmas. In recent years it raised $60–$70,000. A recent letter is shown in full in Appendix D. The letter illustrates some of the elements of the self-portrait. For example, the letter points out that "because it is a private, non-profit agency, YEA has been able to respond with *flexibility* to these [changing] conditions." Most of the letter was devoted to describing YEA's work with one client:

To illustrate how YEA works with a typical youngster, I would like to tell you briefly about a young man (Marvin) who first came to the agency in the Fall of 1968 when he was sixteen, following a term at the N____ H____ Training School for Boys. He had been sent to this state training school because of his long record of school truancy, breaking and entering, and auto theft.

After failing on many jobs, and after "many hours of counseling," the client was said to "rank high" in a training program where he had been placed. The letter continued:

This story of Marvin exemplifies the basic purposes of YEA. First, of course, is the commitment to help the youngster stand on his own feet and develop a mature attitude toward himself through a positive work experience. Marvin required a long time to reach this point—which is not unusual considering his age and his background. What is unusual and makes YEA unique is the *continuing availability of the agency's services* during this developmental process.

The letter concludes by noting that while the agency received funds from government sources, "the lifeblood of YEA is the support it receives from individuals, corporations, and foundations."

In a four-page document prepared in early 1973, as part of a contract proposed to Center City's Narcotic Rehabilitation Agency, YEA portrayed itself to this funding organization in much the same way (without, of course, mentioning the importance of private money).

For over 30 years, YEA has demonstrated *leadership, effectiveness, efficiency* and *ingenuity.* In early 1940 YEA was one of the first private or public agencies to attack the problem of black unemployment. In the 1950's YEA developed its City-wide reputation as the *"no red-tape" organization* which can make placements too difficult for other agencies. YEA has always operated efficiently—the agency's Cost-per-Placement is thought to be the lowest in the city. In 1968, YEA pioneered an on-the-job training program which opened many architectural firms to young Center City dropouts . . . . The ability to provide *"instant action"* for its youngsters stems from YEA's long standing relationship with over 800 companies which know the agency, trust its counselors, and take its youngsters.

A recent brochure had a photo of a black youth on the cover, working earnestly with pencil and paper. Inside the brochure, additional characteristics of the "unplaceable clients" are provided, but they are merely "so-called unplaceable" because of the unique traits of YEA. "Youth Employment Agency is special because its innovative approaches to finding jobs for 'unemployable' youth enable it to function more effectively, more efficiently, and at a fraction of what it costs public agencies."

An even more recent brochure had a different tone. Clients are described as being young, with less emphasis on their criminal and drug backgrounds. Even the agency is not described in such heroic terms. However, the main elements of the self-portrait remain, even though they are presented in a more matter-of-fact manner.

Because YEA is private, it is flexible enough to respond quickly to the needs of youths and to changes in the labor market. Over forty years' experience has made us not only effective but economical because we can cut red tape and bureaucracy to the minimum.

Since 1936, YEA has responded to the needs of youth, rather than to the politics of the day.

THE CLIENTS

There is no single description that covers YEA's clients very well. "Disadvantaged" was a commonly used term and, in its awkward way, covered those shortcomings attributable to poverty and discrimination that manifested themselves as illiteracy, a low level of work motivation, and an outlook on the world comprised of cynicism and hope (in about equal measure). However, the term does not cover the range of client types found at YEA, nor does it convey to the reader a sense of what the clients were actually like, and thus what the counselors were faced with. The first of the following agency reports presents some of the categorical dimensions of the clientele. The second report approaches the problem from the standpoint of personal characteristics, but still in the form of central tendencies. The case histories that follow are then used to show that the clients were not all alike but came in a variety of combinations. For the working counselor, there was no standard client and uniform intervention. The client was a puzzle to the counselor.

In August 1975, the executive director presented to the executive committee of the board of directors a study of the characteristics of the client population at that time. The board was interested in whether the agency was ranging too far above its traditional age range (16–21) and whether it was placing clients who did not really need help in securing employment.

The findings reported by the director were based on a survey of clients seen between November 1, 1974, and June 30, 1975. The survey showed that 60 percent of the clients were 16–19 years of age, 70 percent were male, 68 percent had either a correctional or a narcotic history, 78 percent had not graduated from high school, 29 percent had no previous work experience, and 93 percent were "members of the Hispanic or Black minorities."

"There were some people placed, who *might* have been able to find jobs on their own," the report noted, but they "were certainly in the minority" and were probably due to "a 'contamination' factor in the screening of applicants by the referral agencies, and in the recruitment done for OJT." The director concluded that "YEA *is* very clearly serving the 'hardest to place' despite the suggestion of 'playing the numbers game.' "

Clients were characterized in other ways as well. The report submitted to the funding agency for the addict program in September 1974 illustrates this.[9] The report reviewed the list of acceptable reasons for refusing to enroll clients in the program. Among the reasons listed are "serious lack of motivation, as revealed in the assessment interview," failure to keep appointments, poor appearance, rejection of reasonable job offers, and "other conditions not listed above, which seriously impair the ability of the client to participate successfully in the program and/or obtain employment."

This list reflects the anticipated qualities of the clients at the beginning of the addict program, based on YEA's experience with such clients. Besides those qualities discussed earlier (educational level, narcotics usage, and so on), clients were seen as possibly lacking motivation, lacking discipline (keeping appointments), presenting a poor appearance, and being unrealistic in their job requirements.

The report then proceeded to analyze a sample of 133 clients rejected by the addict program staff. In this sample, 22 clients were rejected for "lack of motivation" or "attitudinal problems"; 20 clients were rejected for failure to keep appointments or maintain contact with the counselors; two clients "turned down jobs commensurate with their skills"; and 25 clients were rejected for unspecified reasons.[10]

The report also offered data on "job terminations" for clients who were accepted into the program and placed on jobs in the October 1973–mid-April 1974 period. There were 308 placements made during this period; 66 of these placements resulted in "terminations." Of those who were terminated, 26 quit their jobs, 23 were fired, 4 were laid off, and 13 had been placed on temporary jobs to begin with.

The evidence suggests that there are some differences between those who quit their jobs and those who are fired. Of the 26 who quit, 10 did so to "advance to a better position," and 8 did so because of "poor employer-employee relationships" which in some cases appeared to reflect unfair treatment by employers. The 23 clients who were fired, on the other hand, were fired because of "lack of motivation, interest, or initiative," poor work performance, absence or lateness, and "evidence of drug usage." The cases were distributed fairly evenly among these reasons.

Thus, approximately half of the clients who were placed appear to exhibit many of the same characteristics as those who were rejected by the program. These characteristics include general lack of job readiness (or motivation), absence and lateness, and unrealistic expectations. This group of clients, however, was put into a new situation (work) which brings out additional shortcomings: poor work performance and personal conflicts with employers. Some clients were "transient" and some return to using narcotics.

It is not possible to analyze this material in any greater detail. The person who was ostensibly fired for poor work performance may also have been late frequently and dissatisfied with his position. Nor should one conclude that all clients were deficient in all the ways that the report cited. It can only be said that, as a group, clients were seen as being "hard to place" for these reasons—and when placed they frequently were not satisfactory workers for many of the same reasons that made initial placement difficult.

Analysis of a sample of YEA's case files shows both the importance of a job's being available and the variability of the clientele. Some clients were quickly placed when a suitable job was available. In some cases, this was repeated again and again over several years' time. These might be called "professional" clients.

The number of professional clients is relatively small. However, the type represents to an extreme degree other clients who return several times for job placement over a period of 2 to 3 years. The agency does not discourage such dependence until it becomes obviously out of place, even absurd (as the following case illustrates). Professional clients are good for scoring placement successes. Also, they seem to *want* to be helped and stimulate the counselor's *desire* to help. It is difficult for counselor and client to break the relationship once it develops.

One professional client (Case No. 103) is a black male born in Augusta, Georgia, on May 5, 1952. At the time he was first seen at YEA, he was 16 years old. He was a Juvenile Bureau client and had been in two juvenile correctional facilities. In addition, he had a robbery case pending at some time during the course of his involvement with YEA. His IQ was said to be 76, based on tests administered at YEA, though there is reason to believe, based on counselor comments and placement history, that his intelligence was normal. He was first seen at YEA during September 1968 and was seen last almost exactly six years later. During that time he was referred to 21 full-time jobs and was placed on 11 of them. One job lasted for two years, another for eight months. In addition, he was referred and placed on 20 "day jobs," one-day jobs usually involving delivery work. The counselor entries record 49 interviews with the client. The client's folder at the agency was an inch thick. Following are a few of the counselor's notes in this record, beginning with the optimistic entry following the first visit and ending with the anger and rejection shown in the last entries six years later.

COUNSELOR ENTRIES ON M.S. (CASE NO. 103)

9–11–68	Alert neat 16-year old; mature for age. 3 r's are fair—good. Would be eligible for OJT but prefers full-time job now, as he may be returning to school in a month or so.
9–12–68	Mrs. Z__ [employer] likes client. Very pleasant. Will have to be patient with him.
10–24–68	Let go from last job. Didn't really want it. Nice boy but *immature*. Needs firm hand but really has an alertness when probed.
10–29–68	Came in at 9:30. Turned down delivery job.
8–6–69	Worked at B__ T__ Company for 6 months. Also worked for R__ S__ Company. Went away for one month and has worked off and on since then. Is married now and wife expects baby in Dec. '69. No jobs available at the time.
12–24–69	Lost his job on account of lateness and absence. Immature. Wants something big.
2–24–70	Has been drifting. Doing odds and ends jobs: delivery, etc. Should be tested. Does have potential. Trying to find himself. See ref.
11–29–73	M__ was in late for his appt. today. He has to go to Family Court tomorrow and has a criminal case pending for around

	Jan. 1. For these reasons, he was not sent out to a job today. He will return on Monday, Dec. 3 for placement.
6–24–74	M__ was in to YEA today to say he had been laid off last job due to an absence. He was talked to at length concerning the importance of him trying to hold a job. Today he was sent out to temporary work.
9–11–74	M__ walked in today asking for F/T work. Once again it has been stressed to him that he must hold on to the jobs that YEA gets him. It is contrary to his interests to "job hop" and therefore extend his unstable work history. M__ was sent to a F/T job today.
9–16–74	M__ called in to YEA from S__ N__ Company saying that he does not want to work here because of the low salary and the type of labor involved. Both of these conditions were explained to him in full before he was sent to the job interview. M__ agreed to take it at that time. Due to M__'s age [22] and his repeated inability to hold a F/T job, it is now recommended that YEA discontinue servicing M__. It is judged that his best interests demand that he look for work on his own and not have YEA to continually fall back upon for more temporary work. With this crutch removed, it is hoped that M__ will learn to hold on to future jobs made available to him.
9–24–74	The client was seen by C__ F__ [counselor] today. He complained about the way he was being serviced and he wanted to be referred to another job today. No suitable openings were available and job referral couldn't be made. He was asked to telephone C__ G__ on 9/25.
9–25–74	Client returned to office instead of calling. No suitable openings were available again today. The client became angry over this. In view of his attitude and his age, he was told that he could no longer be serviced by YEA.

If professional clients have voluminous records, the records on "ideal" clients are sparse and consist mostly of the forms filled out in the registration process. They see a counselor, are placed on a job on the first referral, and remain on the job—often for some time. It is almost too easy for the counselor. But we must remember that luck plays a part: A suitable job has to be available.

Case No. 84 is a black male who was 19 years old at the time he was first seen at YEA. He was referred by the crime-prevention program and was on a methadone maintenance program as well. He was incarcerated for a misdemeanor; the specific offense was not recorded. He completed the 9th grade before dropping out of school. His IQ was measured as 78. Reading skills were assessed as being at the 5.7th grade for word meaning and 4.8th grade for paragraph comprehension. His math proficiency was at the 2.9th grade level, according to the test used.

The client was registered at the agency in March 1976. He saw a counselor for the first time one day later. The counselor's entry notes:

Client asked about training possibilities. He seems well motivated to do whatever it takes to develop job marketable skills. He is not ready to enter training, however. He is in need of remediation before he could qualify for such a program. He was given an appointment to see the remediation teacher. There were no suitable job openings to offer him today.

Despite this evaluation of the client's training potential, the record shows that the following day he was called and sent out to apply for a job. The job was a "Garnett-machine trainee," a position developed by the OJT staff. The client was hired at $2.50 an hour and started that week. The last entry in the client's folder, dated April 28, said, "Applicant appears to be progressing within the training framework outlined [in the OJT subcontract]. Client attitude seems positive. Employer satisfied with performance to date."

Some clients appear to be better able to handle employer rejection without giving up on their pursuit of a job. We might call these "exemplary" in recognition of their good example in this respect. The exemplary client is referred unsuccessfully several times before he is hired. The referrals usually occur within a relatively short period of time. The client is also willing to accept lesser jobs if necessary and may be the most important kind of client for the counselor, for he is the one who heeds the advice or warnings to "keep in touch."

Case No. 32 is a Puerto Rican male who was 23 years old when he was registered at the agency. He had no "correctional background" or reported narcotic usage. He had obtained his high school equivalency while in the Navy (serving from January to May 1972, and separated with a "General Discharge"). The psychometrist reported that the client had an IQ of 120 and that his reading was at the 11th to 12th grade level. The client's math proficiency was at the 7th grade level.

The client was first seen on July 26, 1972. He was referred unsuccessfully to three jobs: a messenger job and two stock clerk jobs. Then, on August 7, 1972, the client was referred to a porter position. He was hired and began work on August 8. He worked as a porter until October 3; at that time he was accepted into YEA's draftsman-training program. The program combined part-time work in an engineering firm and part-time instruction at YEA's offices. The client was let go by his first employer in this program because he was a slow worker. However, the staff was successful in getting him hired by another engineering firm. He finished the training program in the top third of his class.

For many, however, the lack of a job was a severe test; they became discouraged or disgusted and no longer returned for service. These "discouraged" clients are initially indistinguishable from exemplary ones; both are referred unsuccessfully several times. However, the discouraged client, as the name implies, is unable or unwilling to continue. He does not return to the agency.

An example is Case No. 117, a black male who was 19 years old when he was registered at YEA. He was referred by the youth program and had no correctional or narcotics history recorded. The client was attending school in the evenings, working toward his high school equivalency. His reading ability was described as poor and his math as good by the counselor. The client was not tested by the psychometrist; the counselors had simple tests they used in such cases to get a general idea of the client's reading and math abilities.

This client was registered at YEA in November 1975. The counselor observed that the major obstacle to placement was that the client had "little work background." However, he was described as "neat and suitable for referral," and as being "cooperative, attentive, friendly, and serious." The counselor also recorded that the "client is in school evenings. He has some knowledge of carpentry and electronics from vocational school."

The client was referred to a woodwork trainee position the day he was registered. The counselor recorded that the employer was not hiring at that time, but that he "expects to expand soon," and would keep the client's application on file. The client was not seen again at YEA. In December, the counselor called the client and referred him to a messenger job. He was not hired because the job required him to have his own bicycle. There were no further entries recorded.

During the period of research, however, a great many clients simply did not return to the agency after the initial appointment and interview. Many of these phantom clients may have been discouraged in the interview (this is discussed later); others were probably complying with a parole officer's directive in registering at the agency; still others were either over-qualified for the type of job offered by YEA or were suitably qualified but unwilling to accept the typically low-status jobs.

In all, 12 "types" were derived from the sample of case files. This is neither an exhaustive nor an exclusive classification. But the types do illustrate some of the varieties of clients with which the counselors worked. The types, and a brief description of each, are shown in Table 1.6. The labels given to each are meant to express an important characteristic of each type, but they do not fully describe the type.

Table 1.6
"Client Types" and Their Characteristics

Type	Characteristic
1. Hit and Run	Placement soon after registration; client does not last on job and is not seen again
2. Professional	Long-term involvement with client, often lasting several years.
3. Salesman	Verbal, persuasive client; counselor becomes enthusiastic; client does not return.
4. Ideal	Placement soon after registration; client stays on the job.
5. Exemplary	Client referred several times unsuccessfully; then is placed successfully.
6. Discouraged	Same as "Exemplary," except client "gives up" sooner and is not placed.
7. Fighter	Uncooperative, defiant, and "immature"; argues with counselor, refuses to come in to discuss job openings, etc.
8. Exotic	Unusual appearance or behavior such as flagrant homosexuality, bizarre dress or speech.
9. Leper	Extremely unqualified for most jobs (physical defects, IQ, education, etc.).
10. Slummer	Distinctly over-qualified for agency jobs; some college or technical background.
11. Unrealistic	Qualified for "better jobs" offered by agency (Xerox operator, assembler, etc.) but does not want such low-status jobs.
12. Phantom	Does not return after registration or first counseling session.

NOTES

1. These figures are shown in the *Statistical Abstract of the U.S. 1982–83* (Washington, D.C.: Government Printing Office, 1983), items 566–69.

2. Since then YEA has expanded its clientele to include all youths 16–21 regardless of whether they have arrest or correctional records. Nevertheless, the client population is still heavily weighted with "correctional cases." Until 1975 the agency had a long-standing contract with the state, providing counseling and job placement for youths released from the state training schools.

Other contracts, discussed later, also frequently involved clients dredged up by the criminal justice machinery of the city and state.

3. *Personnel Practices* manual of the agency.

4. *The National Cyclopedia of American Biography* (New York: James T. White, 1960–63 ed.).

5. When the founder's father died, there was a plaque commemorating his service installed at one of the major prisons of the state.

6. The newspaper folded in 1966 while the founder was president.

7. "Their Last Hope—A Job!" *Parade* magazine, March 9, 1969.

8. This and the other quotes interspersed with the description of the daily operations are taken from the *Parade* article cited above.

9. The report covers the contract period September 1, 1973–August 31, 1974.

10. Only two clients were rejected for "returning to drug usage." Fifteen of the clients "found jobs on their own" and were not accepted into the program for that reason.

2

The Counselors

YEA's counselors are the link between the agency and the clients. That link is a strong or a weak one depending, first of all, on the counselors' degree of commitment to the work. The counselors at YEA were not saints. However, they did seem to have an uncommonly strong commitment to their work and, in fact, thought of themselves as "dedicated" to it. The commitment (or dedication) was often expressed in terms of the satisfaction gained from trying to help the clients. This aspect of the counselor's work is discussed here in the context of altruism, a concept that will help to understand the counselors themselves and the rewards of the work, and one that will provide an insight into the significance of certain other developments reported later.

Altruism is selfless behavior, involving a sharing of one's resources and love with others who are unfortunate or "left out" in one way or another. Almost everyone does this at one time or another. Here, however, we want to define a character type, one for whom "concerned" behavior acquires a rather consistent pattern and is manifested in an occupation, a "calling."

Auguste Comte appears to have originated the term. Altruism denoted for Comte "the supreme virtue in the religion of humanity" he was attempting to establish as a rival to Christianity in France. Rooted in the Latin *altrui*, or "other," altruism referred to the discipline and eradication of self-centered desire and a life devoted to the good of others, "more particularly, a selfless love and devotion to society."[1]

In Sorokin's view, we have studied "the negative types of human beings sufficiently—the criminal, the insane, the sinning, the stupid, and the selfish. But we have neglected the investigation of the positive types of Homo sapiens—the creative genius, the saint, the 'good neighbor.'"[2]

Using a sample of "good neighbors" and Christian-Catholic saints, Sorokin studied their age, sex, social class, and the paths they followed to become good neighbors or saints. Although "good neighbors" were largely business and professional persons, their parents were to a great extent (58 percent) from the "farm and industrial labor classes." On the other hand, "some 62 percent of the saints came from the ranks of royalty and the upper nobility strata."[3]

Most good neighbors "had gradually and quietly grown into altruists from early childhood, without any notable catastrophe or other event to mark a sharp turning point in their life." These were called the "fortunate altruists." The others experienced a "turning point marked with a definite 'unusual' experience that divided their life into two different parts: sinful and selfish before the unusual experience, and saintly and unselfish after it."[4] These were the "catastrophic altruists." Among these catastrophes were "death of loved ones" and "illness of the good neighbor."

For saints, it seemed that "catastrophic" or unusual events were more important in their development than in the development of "good neighbors," though the large majority appear to have developed under less dramatic circumstances. However, unlike the good neighbors, the catastrophes described for saints seldom seemed to involve personal tragedies and grief. Rather, they were more often uplifting experiences (sermons, for example). Saints may have suffered for their beliefs, but apparently they did not become saints *because* of any great personal suffering. Good neighbors, on the other hand, were sometimes converted to goodness because of personal suffering.

In general, good neighbors and saints appear to be different in several respects, as shown in the following table.

	Good Neighbors	Saints
Stratum	Middle	Upper
Parental Stratum	Lower (over half)	Upper
Percentage of "Fortunates"	97% or less	78–82%
Percentage of "Catastrophics"	3% or more	18–22%
Experience of "Catastrophics"	Suffering	Uplifting

Elsewhere Sorokin has suggested five variables involved in altruistic love, and some ways in which the variables are correlated.[5] Such love can vary according to its extensity, its duration, its intensity, its purity, and the adequacy of its objective manifestation—in relation to its subjective purpose.

The *extensity* of love is a measure of how many one loves, ranging "from the zero point of love of oneself only, up to the love of all mankind, all living creatures, and the whole universe." In between these extremes "lies a vast scale of extensities: love of one's own family, or a few friends, or love of all the groups one belongs to—one's clan, tribe, nationality, religious, occupational, political, and other groups and associations."[6]

The *duration* of love, Sorokin says, "may range from the shortest possible moment to years or throughout the whole life of an individual or of a group."[7] Love of a low intensity may last a short time or a long time, and the same goes for love of a high intensity. However, Sorokin sees a general tendency for high-intensity love to be of short duration: "The great altruists like Jesus, Buddha, St. Francis, Nil Sorsky, and Gandhi are as rare as the greatest genius in the field of truth or beauty."[8] The "great altruists" are those who rank high in all the variables of love.

The *adequacy* of love refers to the congruence (or lack of it) between the intended effects of love actions and the actual effects. In other words, with love, good intentions are not enough. The outcome may even be harmful. In general, Sorokin argues that one cannot effectively love a great many people; the variables tend to constrain each other. These variables are useful in analyzing the work of YEA's counselors, even though we begin by noting three problems, neglected by Sorokin, that were found to be of some importance in this study.

First, Sorokin assumes that the altruist knows what the "love object" wants and needs, and can provide it. This might best be treated as problematic. While many people want and need to be loved, the love object may want more than love: jobs, money, prestige, education, or self-esteem. These must be provided quickly and routinely. When numerous others make the same or similar demands, just how *does* one "love" an object (client) through one's professional activity?

Second, it seems likely that one principle of love is *likeness*. Love of one's tribe or family would seem to imply, at the least, a lesser love for other tribes or families. The basis of the differentiation of objects is not analyzed in Sorokin's work. The question of whether love for different groups is the same as love for one's "own kind" is neglected. In discussing the counselor's relations to clients, it will be helpful to understand whether the counselors liked and responded only to certain clients with certain traits (which appear to have varied from one counselor to the next), and if love for one's "own kind" (for example, black counselors working with black clients) has a different quality than "love" of another kind (as in the case of white counselors and black clients).

Third, certain organizational features tend to limit the expression of altruism and knowledge of the consequences of counselor's actions—thus, knowledge of the objective adequacy of actions. These included, at YEA, growing *specialization* of tasks (especially post-placement counselors, who "took over" after placement and controlled the flow of information from the client), and the *focus of the work* (placement) deriving from organizational definitions, hiring standards, and so on. We might also add *size of caseload* as a factor that may reduce knowledge of the adequacy of one's actions. For these reasons, the altruism of the counselors must be considered alongside other factors such as organizational definitions, client expectations, task specialization, and level of professionalization.

The particular form of altruism observed at YEA can be called "organizational altruism." Its principal features are:

1. Selection of the "objects" (clients) in terms of organizational criteria
2. Enforced interaction between "altruist" (counselor) and "object" by the organization
3. Standards and mechanisms of accountability, with at least some semblance of objective measurements of performance
4. Monetary compensation for altruistic services
5. Limited professionalization of the "altruists"

Organizational altruism can be distinguished from the "professional altruism" discussed by Lubove.[9] The phenomenon of professionalization, so important in Lubove's study of social work, may be less significant when seeking to understand the work of YEA's counselors. In Lubove's work, the principal conflict is between the social worker's eager pursuit of professionalization (based on specialized training) and the more spontaneous (but patronizing) "concern" of the volunteers. At YEA, the conflict appears to be between the constraints principally imposed by the organization and the personal concern of the counselors for their clients. We turn next to some indicators of that concern, followed by an examination of the counselors' statements about the meaning of their work to them.

SOME GRATIFICATIONS OF THE WORK

Is counseling an altruistic occupation? Does it show any signs of being a "calling," not primarily dependent on the usual rewards of jobs (praise, promotion, and so on)? To answer these questions the "meaning" of the work was assessed in the following manner:

1. Counselors were asked about their interest in working in private industry at a higher salary. The question was repeated at different increments above the counselor's present salary, in an attempt to arrive at a "sell-out price."
2. Counselors were also asked about their use of clients' expressions of thanks or praise. The question was designed to ascertain if the praise itself was sufficient gratification, or if counselors attempted to use it for their own advancement by reporting it to superiors.
3. The career patterns of YEA's counselors were analyzed.
4. Counselors were questioned about how they happened to be engaged in the

work, their careers, and their own accounts of the gratifications they obtained from the work. Sometimes these data emerged in response to a direct question. At other times, the information emerged while talking about something else.

SALARIES AS WORK INCENTIVE

It would be unrealistic to expect any profession or calling to offer only the rewards of the work itself. The internal and external rewards of an occupation are not an either-or proposition. The question is: In which direction does the occupation or the person lean? Use of the salary question was intended to provide a rough assessment of altruistic "purity."

Counseling has its external rewards: white-collar work with professional or semi-professional status and prestige, and considerable autonomy in doing the work. Salaries are another external reward. They are not very high, to be sure, when compared with other professional occupations, suggesting either that income may not be the primary inducement or that most of the counselors are not qualified for other, higher paying occupations (or both). The relatively low level of professional education and the class background of YEA's counselors might lead us to expect a greater interest in salary. The counselors typically come from blue-collar families. The reported occupations of fathers included, for example, Transit Authority shopworker, machinist, auto mechanic, barber, and railroad laborer. The interviews suggested, however, that money was not that important to the counselors, even though they were concerned about money and complained about being underpaid. When asked whether they would accept a job in private industry paying more money, most counselors expressed great reluctance even when the increase was $4,000 a year.[10] Above $4,000 most began to waver; but all indicated a strong preference for a similar job.

The counselors' responses to the money question are summarized in Table 2.1. Thus, only one would be tempted by a $500 increase, and two more would be tempted by a $4,000 increase. All felt that the kind of job offered would be an important factor in their decision.

It may be that $4,000 is not sufficient to test the commitment to counseling work. However, in view of the relatively low salaries of the counselors (averaging between $9,000 and $10,000 at the time) their reluctance to leave the job merely for more money seems significant.

THE RESPONSE TO CLIENTS' GRATITUDE

When asked how he would go about letting his supervisor know about thanks received from a client, Counselor A was at first contemptuous

Table 2.1
Annual Salary Increase Necessary for Acceptance of a Job in Private Industry

COUNSELOR	$500	$1000	$2000	$4000
A	NO	NO	NO	NO
B	PROBABLY	YES		
C	NO	NO	NO	"TEMPTED"
D	NO	NO	NO	NO
E	NO	NO	NO	"POSSIBLY"

and proud, saying he would "just let the supervisor judge me by how I produced." Then he added that "if I was working with the type of supervisor who needs this, I would have to find some way to let him know. It's good politics. He should know if he is a supervisor."

Other counselors were more direct in their evaluation of the client's expression of thanks. When asked the same question, Counselor D said: "I get that a lot. But I never say much about it unless it comes in a letter, which we might be able to use for fund raising. I don't go out of the way, though. I just don't feel it's necessary to mention it otherwise." The counselor felt that a call from a client thanking him was "elevation enough—it's just a personal thing."

Counselor C said that she would record the information in the client's folder. She cited two instances of this sort. "I shared them with my supervisor," she added. In response to a direct question about the relative value of praise or gratitude from the client versus praise from her supervisor, she said that "the client calling to thank you means more than praise from the supervisor." Such a response is what we might expect, of course, but it is worth noting nonetheless.

Counselor E responded to the same question by saying that he would bring the praise or thanks to the attention of the referring counselor, but not to his supervisor. His supervisor, he said, had put him down in the past, and he appeared to feel that it would be demeaning to try to show in this fashion how competent he is. "I've gotten hundreds of letters of thanks," he said, but he refused for personal reasons to show them to his supervisor.

Responses to this question were used also to measure the "purity" of the counselors' altruism. Assuming that the clients' expressions of praise or gratitude are unsolicited, we can consider what the counselors do with such unsolicited rewards. Is it sufficient and gratifying in itself? The answer seems to be that in many cases it is not. Only two counselors indicated that the reward would be sufficient and meaningful in itself. The others showed varying degrees of using the praise in various ways.

If we compare these findings with the "salary-increase" question previously discussed, we might conclude that on the combined indicators of altruism, Counselor D ranks the highest on both. Some of those who ranked relatively high on the "salary" indicator do not rank so high on the "gratitude" indicator (Counselor C and Counselor E, for example). And Counselor A showed on both measures a rather individualized response based on such unanticipated factors as his "production," pride, and career interests. Overall, though, he showed clearly a pragmatic attitude: showing the supervisor any letters of praise if the supervisor expected or responded to it. The combined indicators point to one "pure" altruist among the counselors, with lesser degrees of altruism shown by other counselors. However, it seems advisable to interpret responses to the second question with caution. Sharing praise does not necessarily imply an exclusive concern for self-advancement.

COUNSELORS' EMPLOYMENT HISTORIES

Questions about previous jobs and information from the personnel records were meant to provide some indirect measure of the "intensity" of the counselors' altruism.

An attempt was made to find out what kinds of jobs were taken by counselors who had left the agency in the previous four to five years. Only two had gone into private industry, and both of these went to work for an airline as part of a minority-group training program. Most others went to governmental agencies. Two went to a program providing special services for disadvantaged minority-group students in the Center City's public university, one went to the State Narcotics Control Bureau, two went to the State Employment Service, one went to the city's Department of Youth Services, and one went to a church-related narcotics program. Two returned to school for advanced degrees. This consistency probably reflects, to some degree, the limited choices available and the difficulties in transferring to a different field at the same or a higher salary. But an additional factor appeared discernible in counselors' comments during the interviews: As youths (even as a child, in one case) some either had been helped by a counselor, social worker, or similar professional or else, having needed guidance of some sort and not receiving it, they recognized a need to help others.

Little information was available, at the time the study was done, on those who had left recently. One black counselor left to accept a job with a state agency that raised money for the construction of college dormitories. His duties involved seeing that minority-group workers were employed on the construction of the dormitories. Another counselor (white) who was laid off in the spring of 1976 found a position as a teacher in a private school.

Perhaps little can be made of these findings when considered alone, keeping in mind that the availability of positions for counselors is limited by their specialized experience and, in some cases, by limited education ("limiting" either in the sense that they do not have B.A. degrees or because the degree is in a field that is in little demand in business). But the career patterns of counselors support the other findings that suggest a sense of purpose or mission in this type of work— that is, some inner meaning. The jobs counselors had held *prior* to working for YEA also support this interpretation.

When the counselors were asked how they happened to get into counseling, their responses seemed, at first, to suggest highly individualized reasons and random factors.

Counselor A (black male) said that he became a counselor "by accident." He had worked as a computer operator and programmer, employed by a non-profit organization. Then he had a summer job with a large oil company; the job involved staging variety shows in various low-income areas of Center City. "We looked for talent in the communities," the counselor reported. "I enjoyed doing that, working with kids." Then he found out about a job as an instructor for a federally funded training program. That program provided pre-vocational training for the disadvantaged and unemployed. When the program was terminated, he happened to meet YEA's director at a testimonial dinner for a regional Manpower administrator. They had discussed a job at YEA which he eventually accepted. It appeared that this "accidental" opportunity was consistent with a patterned interest that had developed over time, although the level of "intensity" was moderate, from all indications.

Counselor B (black male) cited his experience as a camper as a youth. He "admired the counselors" and liked the idea of helping people. He later worked for a Mission Society, "in a super Boy Scout atmosphere," working with a youth marching band after school hours. Subsequent to that he was on the full-time staff of the Mission Society. Later, he worked in "counseling and group work" for a large anti-poverty organization. This was followed by a position in a federally funded "industrial education" program. "I started at the age of eight dealing with people . . . helping others with their school work . . . . There is a feeling within me that wants to see an individual getting on his feet . . . . Counseling is not just a job."

Counselor C (black female) reported that she had done some teaching in an anti-poverty program for a while after graduating from college. It was a relaxed atmosphere, working on a one-to-one basis. In college, she said, she was interested in sociology and anthropology, but they were not lucrative enough (with a B.A. degree). Counseling was a "compromise choice." She liked the idea of working with people. An advisor in college "tried to interest me in social work, but I saw no chance to do any exploring (in social work)." The counselor added, however, that while she enjoyed the work, she didn't want to stay in it forever. "I really enjoy the *counseling*," she concluded, "speaking to the kids and all that. It is a challenge. But placement is more difficult. You have to depend on the outside [employers] for that."

Counselor D (white male) did not mention employment in response to the question.

I originally wanted to be a School Psychologist. But I had a lack of guidance in school. I did not take certain courses required for a School Psychologist degree . . . . But I wanted to work with people on a one-to-one basis. Vocational Counseling was the only course I could get into without going back too far. It was not my first choice. But I can save a lot of kids from making the same mistakes I made.

This counselor had previously worked at a school for the deaf, a settlement house, and at two institutions for adoptive and foster children. Prior to that, he held two teaching positions and was a caseworker for the city's Department of Youth Services.

Counselor E (Puerto Rican male) worked as a salesman for a time before going to work for a Puerto Rican anti-poverty organization. He reported that he used to make "informal placements" while employed as a salesman and had developed an interest in the work. "Many of my *friends* were in the placement profession." "There was an element of *chance* combined with interest" connected with his entry into counseling, he said. Later in the interview, the counselor expressed a "deep feeling" of satisfaction that he gained from helping others. He said his father used to help others often. "He got kicked in the ass a lot, but he still helped people. I guess this was inculcated in me."

Counselor F (white female) said that she had a friend (Counselor G) who was working at YEA and who told her about an opening for a job developer. She was not considered suitable for that position but was hired as a counselor. This counselor was in a doctoral program (in anthropology) at a local private university. She was not interested in teaching or research but wanted the degree for "credential purposes" in writing non-fiction. She had developed an interest in "one-to-one relationships," she said, as a result of working at YEA. The counselor graduated magna cum laude from a private university, with a major in sociology and anthropology. She had previously worked as an editorial assistant for a big-city newspaper, and as an acting registrar for a school of practical nursing.

Counselor G (black male) said that he got into the field of counseling "by luck and by knowing certain people." His work history, however, suggests a pattern of attempting to break away from social work but returning to it. After graduation from a Texas college he was a social caseworker in Ohio. He then worked as an insurance salesman for two years and then as a "testing specialist" for an Army recruiting station in Rhode Island. Following that, he was an assistant Manpower resource manager in a Model Cities program in Ohio. He went to Center City after that and tried his hand in the theater—"as an actor, a stagehand, anything," but gave up on it. "I was getting too old [29] to be so hungry! If you don't make it big [in the theater] when you're young, it's best to get out. Whereas a job like this [at YEA] is more stable and it's less hectic." This counselor was also in a doctoral program (in sociology) in the same university where Counselor F was enrolled. He did not know what he wanted to do with the degree; however, college teaching did not appeal to him.

Counselor H (black male) refused to talk about any personal matters in the interview. He was only recently employed by YEA. His personnel record shows a pattern similar to that of Counselor G's, a departure and then a return to counseling. His work history shows that he had previously worked first as an employment consultant for a private employment agency, then for an Urban Redevelopment Authority where he "planned community activities, counseled community residents, etc." After that he worked as the supervisor of dispositions in a court. There he "maintained court statistics, visited prisons and interviewed defendants," and directed the pre-trial services program. Subsequent to that he was a broadcast engineer for a Center City TV station and was in a management-training program in a Center City bank. Counselor H has an M.A. degree in public administration.

Counselor J (Puerto Rican male) described in great detail how he came to counseling.

Years ago when I was growing up, there were a lot of people who helped me. If it hadn't been for those people helping me, I wouldn't be where I am—reciprocating what was given to me. The first time I was influenced was—years ago, I was on welfare. And one of the turning points in my life was visiting a welfare office for the first time—just listening to a person—his name was Bob, that was handling my particular case (I was under my mother's welfare thing). Just listening to him—and in terms of what he was able to do—[he] gave me an idea of what I wanted to do. In other words, that's what started me.

The welfare worker, he said, motivated him to think of going to college—"it became a very important thing in my life"—and to want to "get off welfare."

The counselor also described his later experiences working in a local anti-poverty organization: "There I was exposed to the other elements of anti-poverty programs that I really didn't like," he said. The staff was "motivated toward monetary gains more than anything else," partly because "the people were put in a situation where they're earning salaries they've never earned before" and as a result "they tend to become more involved with the salaries they're earning than with their purpose or function."

The counselor went on to describe his subsequent work with the Mayor's Office of Volunteers, where he interviewed people who wanted to do volunteer work and referred them to various agencies. It involved "working with all kinds of people, from middle class to upper class, all kinds of races, colors, and creeds . . . . It really motivated me more . . . . "

When he first applied to YEA for a job as a counselor, he was accepted as a job developer instead. This experience, he said, showed him "the other side of the coin, which was the employer." Eventually, "there was an opening for a counselor here, and I was given the position."

Based on the counselors' personnel records and the information regarding their careers obtained directly from the counselors, the counselors can be classified into four types: fortunates, prodigals, migrants, and converts.

Fortunates were those counselors who seemed to have moved toward the occupation in a steady and apparently uneventful way; in this respect, they resembled Sorokin's good neighbors of this type. These counselors may have recalled good role models early in life or favorable experiences related to helping others, but did not report "conversion experiences" that suddenly influenced their lives. Counselors B, C, and D were considered to be of this type.

The *prodigals* are those who return to counseling after a period of doubt, denial, and exploration of other occupations. They begin their careers in "social work" (in the generic sense) and return to it. Counselors G and H are considered to belong to this group. Counselor H, though he did not wish to answer "personal" questions, had an employment history that fit this pattern.

Migrants are those who over a period of years and a succession of different jobs appear to have been "working toward" counseling work. Their interest develops gradually over a period of time. There is an aspect of each job that seems to lead to the next job. This is seen in the careers of Counselors A and E.

Converts are those counselors who reported specific experiences that appear to have changed their lives. Counselor J and his experience with a social worker exemplify this most clearly. Counselor B might be included here; however, only because he appeared to be alluding to several such experiences, beginning with his camp experiences, we have classified him as a "fortunate" altruist. Counselor F is included in this group because it appeared that her present job (her first one in "social work") seems to have been a conversion experience in itself. Getting the job was something of an "accident." But she talked at length about the "elation" and "powerful" effects obtained from placing certain clients on jobs, and highly valued the "sharing" of intimate experiences with clients.

In summary form, the classification of the counselors into these four types is shown as Table 2.2. Prodigals and converts were subsequently considered to exhibit altruism of a greater "intensity." However, since this part of the study was exploratory, there were no firm criteria established at the outset for classifying the groups.

MEANING OF WORK TO COUNSELORS

There are some obvious disadvantages to using counselors' statements about their work and their expressions of its meaning for them. Foremost among these is how to interpret such statements—if we should assume that counselors think they are supposed to be committed to their work or wish to convince themselves. We might in that situation expect a barrage of high-sounding and self-righteous statements. This possibility cannot be eliminated, although we have attempted, through the presentation of more "objective" data such as employment histories, to reduce this kind of error. Nevertheless, such statements are useful. It is only when counselors are encouraged to talk about their work that one gets a sense of its meaning to them.

The interviews convey a sense of the inner meaning of the work to some counselors, especially of the convert and prodigal types. They indicate that the "altruism" of counselors is focused upon selected individuals rather than upon all clients. The favored clients are those who demonstrate motivation by keeping in touch or those who somehow "touch" a counselor by, for example, resembling the counselor himself

Table 2.2
Distribution of Types among Counselors

FORTUNATES	PRODIGALS	MIGRANTS	CONVERTS
Counselor B	Counselor G	Counselor A	Counselor J
Counselor C	Counselor H	Counselor E	Counselor F
Counselor D			

as a youth. Counselors are thus able to maintain a continuity and intensity of altruism. In doing so, they in part meet organizational demands that they interact with an *extensive* group. Some excerpts from selected interviews follow.

From the Interview of Counselor J

When this counselor was asked, "What are some important qualities for a counselor to have?" he talked about understanding one's own limitations, treating each client as an individual despite a pressure to stereotype them, and the need for keeping abreast with changes in the external world, such as in the job market. Then he added, "Also, I think you really have to—not *like* what you're doing [but] *love* what you are doing." Asked how he dealt with the frustration of not being able to do something for everybody who came into his office, he replied:

That's where the *love* comes in . . . . It's difficult dealing with the frustration. But I think the satisfaction of *one kid* calling back, ecstatic that he's got a job— I think that holds you, in terms of what you think may be failures in other areas, not being able to place all of them.

The counselor's feeling for the clients appeared to be based in part on his own experiences: "It's like looking into a mirror and seeing yourself. You see kids and you remember when you were young."

The gratification appears to be partly narcissistic: "You can see a large portion of yourself in them, and in some sense it brings you closer to yourself." Counseling can be an "ego booster," the counselor said, "but at the same time, you know you're helping in some sense."

From the Interview of Counselor F

This counselor, a white female, was asked what she would miss most about the job if she left it. She replied:

The clients mostly. The new people coming in—it's quite an adventure, meeting new people, having the time to talk, etc. And then you'd miss the ones you're already working with, whether they're working on jobs or you're working on placing them. But the clients is the main thing I would miss. There's an incredible feeling of accomplishment for me when something works.

She cited as an illustration a case where she had problems getting a client placed. She had to do some "special solicitation" for him—calling various employers to find a job for the one client.

Finally, he got the job. I was walking home after work and I discovered I was feeling very elated. For a second, I couldn't think why. I thought it was something special that happened on my lunch hour or that my boyfriend had called me during the day. Then all of a sudden I zeroed in on it, and I realized that I was ecstatic for Ted [the client]! And when that happens, it's really powerful! It's just as if you had done it yourself. Just as if you had gone out and gotten the job. I've been through unemployment myself, had very hard times, and I know that feeling when you've had a good interview, or especially when you've been hired.

From the Interview of Counselor G

The counselor, a black male, was asked, "What gives you satisfaction on your job?" He replied:

Any time I can place a kid on a job, I'm satisfied. There are satisfactions in other ways—in offering a kid, a lot of kids, information they will never have before. Factual information. Insights I don't aim for. That's a waste of time. I don't see where I'm going to get all this wisdom suddenly, when I couldn't apply it to my own life.

Among the important qualities for a counselor to have, he noted, "You gotta like people. All kinds." When asked if he ever got any clients he did not like, he replied:

Yeah, yeah. But then a counselor has to realize there are people he can't like and there are people he can't work with. I find I can't work with subtle kids. I can work better with manipulative kids. Sometimes they have both drives. I find the manipulative kids have a goal, and if it's necessary to manipulate a bunch of bureaucrats to attain the goal, they go out and do it. They don't look at bureaucrats as some holy person . . . .

The counselor appeared to accept certain kinds of clients as they were:

I had one kid, he was making out all right on the street—he ran into his parole officer. The parole officer said, "What are you doing [these days]?" The kid said, "Nothing." He was happy! They [parole officer] sent him right here to [YEA]. And the kid was hurt. I could never send him out to a job. He would never go. But he made the rounds.

When asked how he dealt with such clients, he replied, "I tell them, 'If you don't want to work, and you just want to come here and fool your parole officer—fine! Come in and fool him.' Let him [parole officer] come up with his own conclusions."

Several similar stories were reported by this counselor. It appeared that in such ways he shielded clients from the pressure to work if they were not ready, relying on the client's assessment of his own needs.

When we attempted to understand the "converts" better by using

Sorokin's distinction between uplifting experiences and personal misfortune as one difference between saints and good neighbors respectively we could come to no simple conclusion. For example, Counselor J's admiration of a social worker at the age of 14 would appear to be an uplifting experience; however, the fact that he and his mother were on welfare may be considered personal misfortune. Which is decisive? Similarly, Counselor F's exposure to the "elation" of placing clients would be uplifting, but it was elating partly because she had been through the misfortune of unemployment herself and could identify with the client because of this.

We were able to discern some connections between level of altruism and career types, and paternal occupation. Again, the findings were not altogether clear insofar as their meaning is concerned. As a whole, the counselors more resembled Sorokin's good neighbors than his saints, with respect to the social stratum of their parents as measured by paternal occupation. Table 2.3 shows these occupations and how they are related to the counselors' levels of altruism and their career types.

It seems advisable to refrain from further analysis of this material. The important point is that while most of the counselors can be considered altruistic—helping us understand their commitment to the clients and also their conflicts with the board of directors—at the same time, they vary in the intensity and purity of their altruism. Without this insight we would find certain practices (described later), such as the weeding out of clients and their adjustment to this pragmatic necessity, to be inexplicable.

To summarize briefly, the interviews and other data appear to support the view that the work of helping the clients (in various ways) has an important meaning to the counselors and offers a type of satisfaction probably different from that provided by many other (perhaps most) jobs. There appear to be both an emotional and a moral gratification in helping others who are defined as needing and deserving help. There are other rewards evident: One counselor refers to the work as an "ego-booster"; another refers to a "sense of accomplishment." In other words, there are certain kinds of ego gratifications as well. But the heart of the work appeared to be the desire to help the client. Why this should be so is not completely explainable on the basis of this data. We have seen some evidence that counselors recognize themselves in the clients and respond to this reflective image. Even for Counselor F, a white woman working with black male clients, identification may be based on "unemployment" or the "desperation" of the client. We can also distinguish between an altruism based on accepting the object of its ministration "as is" and an altruism based on the desire of improving that object by proselytizing, uplifting, or transforming it. Counselor G exemplifies the former type; the other counselors fall into the latter category.

Table 2.3
Characteristics of YEA Counselors, by Father's Occupation

COUNSELOR	SEX	ETHNIC GROUP	FATHER'S OCCUPATION	LEVEL OF ALTRUISM	CAREER TYPE
			WELFARE		
J	Male	Puerto Rican	Lived with mother on welfare	High	Convert
			UNSKILLED AND SEMI-SKILLED LABOR		
A	Male	Black	Railroad laborer	Medium	Migrant
E	Male	Puerto Rican	Machine operator (factory)	Medium	Migrant
			SKILLED LABOR		
B	Male	Black	Mechanic	High	Fortunate
D	Male	White	Barber	High	Fortunate
			WHITE COLLAR		
C	Female	Black	Clerical (municipal transit system)	Low	Fortunate
			OWNERS		
G	Male	Black	Grocery store owner & "numbers"	High	Prodigal
F	Female	White	Furniture store owner	High	Convert

NOTE: No Information was Obtainable on the Occupation of Counselor H's Father.

Counselors seemed to focus their attention only on certain clients. Even Counselor G preferred not to work with "subtle kids." Others withheld attention, time, and "attachment" to the client until he had offered evidence of his motivation. Some clients appeared to touch the counselor by revealing themselves as being prior images of the counselors. But even they had to demonstrate "motivation."

NOTES

1. See Joseph Allen Matter, *Love, Altruism, and World Crisis: The Challenge of Pitirim Sorokin* (Chicago: Nelson-Hall Co., 1974), p. 91. Matter cites an article

by Louis Budd which appeared in *American Quarterly*, vol. 8 (1956), pp. 40–52.

2. Pitirim A. Sorokin, *Altruistic Love* (Boston: Beacon Press, 1950), p. vi.

3. Ibid., p. 123.

4. Ibid., p. 59.

5. Pitirim A. Sorokin, *The Ways and Power of Love* (Boston: Beacon Press, 1954), p. v.

6. Ibid., p. 16.

7. Ibid.

8. Ibid., p. 21.

9. Roy Lubove, *The Professional Altruist* (New York: Atheneum, 1973).

10. This question was not asked in the later interviews. The point seemed well established by the earlier interviews, and since new questions were added to the interview guide it was concluded that this question could be eliminated (in that form, at least) to make time available for other questions. For two reasons, this may have been an error: (1) Personnel changes may have resulted in different responses, and (2) later counselors may have been more willing to take private industry jobs. However, there is still reason to believe that money is not normally a major inducement in attracting people to this work.

3

The Practice of Counseling

Viewing the counselors from the standpoint of altruism, as was done in Chapter 2, is helpful but incomplete. Since the counselors practiced, in an organizational setting, an occupation that has some of the elements of a profession, we must say something about these to draw a more complete picture.

VOCATIONAL COUNSELING AS A PROFESSION

Vocational counseling can be called a profession if we say that to be a profession an occupation must satisfy at least the first six of the following conditions:

1. An *area of specialization* not claimed exclusively by another occupation
2. A *body of knowledge* covering theory of the profession and principles and techniques of practice
3. Some form of *specialized training* beyond the B.A. degree, in the course of which a specialized technique is acquired
4. Some form of *professional association* that grants a meaningful certification to its members
5. A *code of ethics* regulating, or promulgating principles for the self-regulation of, professional conduct and reflecting a collectivity orientation
6. A *professional communications system*, usually in the form of journals, dealing with technique and theory (rather than trade gossip, and so on)
7. *Monopoly or near-monopoly of jobs* by the professional association, a measure of the profession's power in the scenario of history
8. *Control over entry into the profession* by limiting the capacity of training facilities[1]

Using these indicators, the professional status of vocational counseling is summarized in the following table.

Characteristic	Applies to Vocational Counseling?
1. Area of specialization	YES
2. Body of knowledge	YES
3. Professional training	YES
4. Professional association	YES
5. Code of ethics	YES
6. Professional communications network	YES
7. Monopoly of jobs	NO
8. Limitation of training opportunities	NO

The occupation thus possesses six of the eight attributes of a profession. This ignores the relative weight or importance of the individual items. For example, the monopoly of jobs and limitation of opportunities for entry may be the most significant factors in assessing widespread acceptance of an occupation as a full-fledged profession, and in achieving professional power, and may distinguish the strong from the weak professions. However, they are considered here as additions to the basic requirements of professionalization.[2]

The area of specialization claimed by vocational counseling (or guidance, as it is sometimes called) is in rendering assistance to individuals making an occupational choice. The process involves providing information about jobs and work, assessing the abilities and interests of the client, and working out an acceptable occupational plan. The plan may focus on career or more immediate goals, and counseling may culminate in job placement, consistent with the plan developed.

The body of knowledge claimed as its own (item 2) by the counseling profession is of only limited exclusiveness to that profession. The profession borrows heavily from other disciplines, especially psychology and, to a lesser extent, sociology. Like education, from which it also borrows, it applies the knowledge and techniques of other disciplines to its own problems to develop its special body of knowledge. Most of the research reported in the professional journals is oriented toward helping the practitioner. The one subject on which some autonomous research has been undertaken is in the area of development of vocational choices, studying the sequence and characteristics of the process. There appears to be no one theory followed by all practitioners (not unlike the social sciences and other human-services professions). Thus each counselor can, and perhaps must, construct a somewhat unique body of knowledge based on concepts borrowed from psychology, sociology, social work, psychiatry, encounter therapy, and so on that are thought to be useful, given the conditions. For the profession as a whole, the experience of doing counseling and placement provides a unique body of knowledge not derived from one's formal education. Research and experience over time yield information not directly and wholly useful to any other profession.

The academic training available to would-be practitioners in this field leads to a Master's degree. The program usually includes two years of full-time work. There are occasional evening programs but (as in social work) the preferred program requires full-time study, since field experience or internship in an operating agency is desired. Professional training beyond the Master's degree is usually related more to "social welfare," program planning, and administration than to the practice of counseling.

The American Personnel and Guidance Association (APGA), with its specialized divisions, is the dominant professional association. The National Vocational Guidance Association is one division. Its membership is made up largely of school guidance counselors, both high school and college, but includes agency counselors as well. Another division is the National Employment Counselors Association, for "people who counsel in an employment setting" or "those employed in related areas of counselor education, research, administration, or supervision in business and industry, colleges . . . and federal and state governments."[3] A third professional association, for rehabilitation counselors, is the National Rehabilitation Counseling Association. The APGA itself is a fourth organization; however, its interests are broader and more diversified, including personnel workers in industry as well as school guidance counselors, government workers, and agency practitioners.

The "certification" granted by these associations, in the form of membership certificates, is less meaningful than in some other professions. Social workers, for example, have succeeded in making membership in and certification by the American Society of Case Workers a prevalent job requirement. The most significant certification in all professions is the state license to practice. Except for psychologists (in some states), this is not required for non-medical professionals in the "helping" professions, such as counseling in its various forms.

Professional codes of ethics, especially for the medical and legal professions, were designed to provide rules of conduct for independent practitioners. Counselors are not usually independent practitioners; rather, they are employees of a bureaucratic organization. There is some question as to whether a code of ethics is needed or can be applied in such a setting.[4] Despite this problem, an ethical code has been included among the professional criteria here because (1) it is commonly regarded as one of the hallmarks of a profession, and (2) it serves as an indicator of the collectivity orientation of an occupation.

A "professional communications system," including journals, conventions, and papers, is as much an assertion of professionalism as it is an indispensable condition. For vocational counseling the "claim" may be even more important than the nominal function, since it is not one of the old established professions and since, as noted before, the profession borrows most if its basic theory from other disciplines.

Some of the professional journals published for counselors include the *Journal of Employment Counseling*, which publishes articles "illuminating theory or practice in employment counseling"; *The Personnel and Guidance Journal* published by the American Personnel and Guidance Association for counselors and personnel workers in schools, community agencies, government, and business; *The Vocational Guidance Quarterly*, where "manuscripts with meaning for practitioners are preferred"; and the *Journal of Applied Rehabilitation Counseling* which publishes articles that deal with "current theoretical or professional issues, innovative . . . techniques, or research having primary significance for the rehabilitation counselor."

YEA'S COUNSELORS AS PROFESSIONALS

Using the six essential criteria specified earlier, the professionalization of YEA's counselors is summarized in the following table. YEA counselors, by these standards, appear to exhibit only one professional trait. Some confirmation of this assessment is contained in the minutes of a November 1975 meeting of YEA's executive staff: There, the director complained that "our counselors are concerned [too much] with placements. This has been their orientation. We will have to change this in order to survive and justify our existence. Also, the counselors will have to learn to balance *statistics* with *services to clients*."

Characteristic	Possessed by Agency Counselors?
1. Have an AREA OF SPECIALIZATION	YES
2. KNOW AND USE ITS BODY OF KNOWLEDGE	NO
3. Had PROFESSIONAL TRAINING	NO
4. Belong to a PROFESSIONAL ASSOCIATION	NO
5. Know and follow a CODE OF ETHICS	NO
6. Use the PROFESSIONAL COMMUNICATIONS SYSTEM	NO

There is an area of specialization in the counselors' work, namely, services directly related to job placement of "disadvantaged" youth. However, only one counselor had a Master's degree in the field. And it should be clear that without professional training there is no generally accepted "body of knowledge" to speak of available to counselors, beyond what on-the-job training and experience produce. Only one YEA counselor belonged to a professional association (the APGA)—the same counselor who possessed the Master's degree. Finally, with respect to use of the professional journals (the communications system), the library at the agency received most of the journals for use by counselors. According to the librarian, the journals were seldom used. Counselor C remarked that the counseling literature she had read seemed to be "repeating what I already know." This counselor did have some undergraduate counseling courses—more training than most had. She added, "Maybe if I read it a little closer . . . . "

When the counselors at YEA were asked about the ethics of their work, their replies did not suggest a codified body of standards. Counselor A said that there are "professional ethics" involved because "you are dealing with people out of work" and the problem will "get worse as they grow older." Counselor D replied: "Honesty and sincerity. You have to be truthful with the client. Fair but firm. You have to be realistic. And you do not impose your values on the clients." Counselor E said: "You must stay away from employers who specify the race of applicants in their job requirements, and you have to be wary of communicating with employers about the client's past." Counselor F said: "There are lots of little things. Don't keep clients waiting. Don't lead them on about the possibility of a job . . . apologizing to the client for interruptions by other counselors."

The responses of other counselors were similar. By and large, their responses stressed client-centered values which could be summed up by one item in the rather elaborate APGA Code of Ethics for counselors: "The member's *primary* obligation is to respect the integrity and promote the welfare of the counselee or client with whom he is working."[5] The more professional aspects of the APGA code are ignored. The APGA code, for example, calls for the member to "foster the development and improvement of his profession," to accept "a responsibility to the institution within which he serves," to "expect ethical behavior" among colleagues, and not to "seek self-enhancement through expressing evaluations or comparisons damaging to other ethical professional workers." YEA's counselors, by contrast, emphasized the client almost exclusively. The counselor had to be honest (with the client, though not the employer), fair, considerate of the client, aware of his or her own values so as to not impose them on the client, and so on. No concern was evident for more "professional" matters—advancing the profession, collective identification with other professionals, and the independent point of view of the professional (with respect to the organization).

THE RECRUITMENT OF COUNSELORS

When the associate director was hiring staff for a new program in 1976, he was asked what qualities he was looking for in the prospective counselors. The associate director responded, "I don't know exactly what I look for; you ask me what I'm looking for and I don't know!" His arms flew up, a gesture of the hopelessness of explaining it. Earlier, he had said that he tried to get the "general all around feel" of the person being interviewed. Then in discussing it further he mentioned some of the specific qualities he looked for and how he measured them. The traits he mentioned were personality, the ability to get along with others on the staff, the absence of "hangups," general alertness, experience, and "what he can bring to the agency." Conspicuously absent were professional training and knowledge of theory and technique. The associate director was asked, during a later conversation, if he ever talked about technique or counseling theory during interviews. "Yeah, I get around to that," he said. "Sometimes I talk too much. But it's not a full orientation or anything. I try to give them a general idea of what a counselor does here."

The prospective counselor was not asked about *his* approach to counseling. If anything of this nature was discussed, it was in the form of an explanation or description of how the agency approached counseling, especially its emphasis on placement. The associate director also made a point of describing good candidates for the new project as being "members of a team, not one doing this, another one that." In short, employees were conceived as being somewhat interchangeable; so much so that there was, later, a problem of assigning the good candidates to staff slots and figuring out who would do what. "All-around ability" is one answer to the question, What can he bring to the agency? Considering the size of the agency and its lack of resources in relation to needs, a versatile person was more useful and could be more easily shifted to another contract or position later if need be. Counseling theory and technique were not regarded as important.

Of four applicants interviewed during a one-week period, he rejected two immediately. One was rejected because he seemed to have "too many hangups." The other rejected applicant was seen as having insufficient experience (he had recently started on a job) and for "just not making a good impression." The applicant was small and quiet, but there was nothing specifically wrong with him. He had just not projected the right "image." He was lackluster.[6]

The two applicants who were accepted did not have exceptional credentials. Both were college graduates; one had done some post-graduate work but not in a Master's program. And neither had the professional degree. On the other hand, one of the rejected applicants did have a Master's degree and rather extensive experience. The other rejected applicant had a B.A. in sociology.

Experience was not all that important either. One of the accepted applicants had no more related experience than the rejected applicants did. The other accepted applicant did have extensive experience in the field: He had been director of an industrial education project with a staff about the same size as YEA's. But it was his personal qualities that impressed the associate director.

In general, it seemed that experience was not the most important factor. Personality and intelligence seemed to be more important. Self-selection to do work appropriate to the agency brought the candidate to the agency in the first place. Thereafter the agency guided the performance of the counselors—who were chosen for qualities that would, among other things, lead them to accept and use the agency's definition of its mission in their work. The requirements of "concern" and "realism" were both necessary for the agency's purposes—as was versatility, an ability and willingness to switch jobs as needed. "Concern" reflected a feeling for the clientele, but also rendered certain conditions of the work (such as salaries) relatively unimportant, and made organizational constraints such as the contract requirements and the dominance of the board more acceptable. In the end, however, concern and realism seemed to be, if not contradictions at least in perpetual tension.

That formal credentials were relatively unimportant in the hiring and evaluation of personnel is seen also in another case. The associate director was asked his opinion of some of the personnel on staff at the time. His remarks are summarized below.

Counselor G	He's very good. A *thinker*; but lazy.
Counselor H	I have a very high opinion of him. He *keeps busy*.
Counselor J	I would give him a good rating. He is *concerned*. Also a very nice guy.

The associate director also commented, in this conversation, on one of the job developers on the staff. The job developer was described as someone who "did not have a good resume" when he applied for the job. "But I was really impressed by him when I interviewed him," the associate director said. He had told the OJT director, "Forget the resume. Just talk to him."

TRAINING OF COUNSELORS

Neither advanced degrees nor specialized training was required for employment at YEA. Of the 13 counselors on whom the information was available, nine did not have an advanced degree. (Four of these did not have even a B.A. degree.) Of the four who did have Master's degrees, only one had a degree in guidance, the "professional" degree.

If counselors at YEA were not *selected* on the basis of "technical and educational standards," there still remains the possibility that the agency "professionalized" its counselors through a program of in-service training—thus making them more employable elsewhere.

YEA's executive staff discussed the topic of "professionalism in the agency" at one meeting. The minutes of the meeting note that "it was stated that at times we are not that careful about training new personnel." Seminars were discussed as a remedy for this. It was agreed that "seminars will be conducted by staff members and outsiders. This will provide general information. New counselors will need a more intensive training mechanism to deal with one-to-one relationships."

The seminars were never set up, and none of the counselors reported any training of this kind. Moreover, the director's plan for seminars focused on the indoctrination and evaluation of the weaknesses of counselors, rather than on the training of them. The meeting of the executive staff on December 16, 1975, discussed the plan of the seminars further. The minutes of that meeting show that the purposes of the seminars were "to see if the general staff and administration are operating toward the same goal; to weed out those staff members who have attitudes that are not compatible with the goals and philosophy of YEA; and to find out if the staff is capable of growing professionally."

The counselors at YEA were asked about their training at YEA—specifically, who trained them, and what the training consisted of. A selection of their responses follows. Since all the responses were essentially the same, there seems no need to show the replies of all the counselors.

Counselor F: It [my training] was pretty bizarre. No one person trained me. My supervisor gave me a few pointers. On one occasion, she went over the *paperwork* requirements. But in terms of actual counseling, I think she hired me because she felt I had a *natural ability* to do it, and she pretty much left me alone. The first week I did not see any clients. Once or twice I sat in her office while she did an intake interview. She kept saying she was going to . . . sit in while I did an interview, during the first weeks, but she never did. I was sort of wishing that she would . . . . She never did. One other thing—I talked to Bob M____ [a counselor] once. I said that the clients seemed very ill at ease during the initial interview. He was really into that—he had some brochures, and been to some seminars—and we sat and talked for a couple of hours. That was a big help. I would say that more than any training I had, that was the best.

Counselor G: The training [I received] was basically mechanical, in terms of office procedures. Nothing to do with the job, if you mean in terms of "social work skills." I came here as a Psychometrist, and got into counseling two months later—having become bored with testing—That was part of my initial interview, that if a counseling job opened, I would be put into it.

Counselor J: I was trained in the *procedures*—filling out a form, what forms to fill out, what procedures to follow. I think it was more training in the procedural aspects of the job than in terms of actual counseling. I think the training comes when you are sitting in that office with the first client—and you're obviously not getting a thing from him, and you start talking to get information from him. I think *this* is the learning process. There's really no other way you can learn it. The job is just *sitting down and understanding people* . . . . I think you can be taught certain practical procedures. For example, explaining to a client how he is to go dressed to a certain job, or being punctual. I mean, this is the sort of thing he could sit down in a room and a computer could spiel out to him. But in terms of actually obtaining information from him . . . I think that just comes naturally from the person—a *natural ability* . . . which cannot be taught anywhere.

What stands out in these quotes—aside from the *procedural* content of the counselors' training—is the absence of any professional orientation as far as training is concerned. Since the agency defined the work in the way it did, the counselors themselves saw little need for specialized training. The work required "natural ability" and common sense. This should not be surprising, since the counselors were not chosen on the basis of their specialized training. Furthermore, through the practice of "weeding out" clients who were not "job ready," there was little need for whatever knowledge might accrue from training.

Note also that two of the counselors began their employment at YEA in other positions, one as the agency's psychometrist (he did not have the usual training for this position) and the other as a job developer. This transferability of personnel is seen as further evidence for the low regard for technical qualifications that characterizes the agency.

Two of the distinctive tasks performed by professional vocational counselors, career guidance and planning, and intervention into "personal problems" affecting employment appeared to be unimportant to the counselors at YEA. One counselor derided the whole notion of career preparation. As for the clients' personal problems, he claimed that he told clients to "take those back to your social worker."

One more illustration of this point: When counselors were asked to describe an ideal program for the agency's clients, and to identify the various professional services that would be needed, most of them specified a number of services—including psychiatrists and social and community workers—indicating that there were serious problems to be dealt with. But only one indicated that the counselors themselves should be professionally trained. Counselor A complained that the agency got the "worst of the litter" for its staff. "They do not seem to feel it is a profession," he said.

These findings appear to be contradicted by the finding that the counselors resisted the limited focus on placement in their work and desired more opportunities for "qualitative work." They apparently did desire more time for qualitative work, that is, more leisurely and thoughtful work with clients. At the same time, they believed that this kind of work could be accomplished without professional training. The heart of the work is impulsive (a genuine desire to help clients), moral (a high degree of honesty with clients), and experiential (learning by doing). Professional training and techniques would be superfluous. The counselors' notion of qualitative work was limited to the short run: They desired more time to get to know the client better, and additional resources such as vocational training and remediation facilities. Helping the client may, in fact, be rewarding only if one gets the chance to know him. Recalling the hiring standards of the agency, it is evident that the counselors would have limited knowledge of "professional skills" and would have little reason to value them since their own employment was not based on possessing such skills.

THE COUNSELOR AT WORK

It would be difficult to typify the working style of the counselors at YEA. Each had his or her own style: pet questions, the presentations of themselves, and so on. However, certain features of the work were found to be common to all, most notably a focus on the immediate task of job placement and an attempt to persuade the client to accept an available job. The following account (of *Counselor D*, June 16, 1976) is selected from the observations made of each counselor.

Counselor D is a white male, in his thirties. He is assigned to the OJT program. He is the only YEA counselor with a graduate degree in guidance. The reader should imagine this counselor as a short, wiry, intense individual who seems to be on the move even while sitting. He speaks rapidly. He darts in and out of the office, tracking down phone numbers, job orders, and so forth. He may (as he does here) be working with more than one client at a time. Though he may seem disorganized, his reputation at the agency is that of a top counselor. We will note that both of the clients he sees here are sent out on job interviews. Both clients in this observation are black males. The time spent on the two clients was two hours, or an average of an hour for each.

As soon as the client is seated, the counselor asks, "Do you have your Social Security card? Are you looking for a summer position?"

Client: A part-time job.
Counselor: What type of work?

Client: Something mechanical.
Counselor: Something mechanical?

The phone rings. The counselor talks briefly with a client and makes an appointment for him to come in Friday. Then he returns to the client in his office.

Counselor: The health field is closed. [Client evidently listed this as one of his interests.] It usually calls for specific experience. There might be a possibility for training.

The phone rings again: S__ C__ (his supervisor) was calling. The counselor says he is busy now and will be in to see her later.

Counselor (to client): I see you have done stock work. What type of work would you like? Are you going back to school in the fall?
Client: Yes.
Counselor: Have you applied to any hospitals [for a job]?
Client: Yes, B____ Hospital and another one.
Counselor: Hospital work is all community-organized now. But I might be able to do something for you in something you have some background in, like stock work. What specific skills do you have in that area? [How to make shipments through] United Parcel Service? Shipping?
Client: I was speaking to a friend [and] she was telling me I could do some volunteer work in a hospital and maybe get hired.
Counselor: Good suggestion. But how is your financial situation?
Client: I need money.
Counselor: That would rule out the volunteer work. What about the stock [clerk] possibility—while you are going to school?
Client: I don't know . . .
Counselor: I will speak to J____ T____ [Counselor A, who is addict program supervisor and coordinator of skills training] about the possibility of training for hospital work—maybe with a stipend. The problem is, skills training here is confined to two programs—the addict program and the crime-prevention program. I can also check with our information service to see what training programs are open [elsewhere]. The main thing is to keep you in school. [Client is attending a two-year college.] How much tuition do you pay?

The client talks about financial aid problems at school. The counselor shows him a copy of *Vocational Training in Center City* (a directory of training facilities published by YEA): "D__ W__ (the information service director) will maybe know of a training program open. What is the minimum [stipend] you can live on?" The client does not know.

Counselor: But keep this job [the stock job] in mind. I did a little research before you came in. With the job market so tight—it's a good job.

The counselor calls the skills-training coordinator and asks about the possibility of training for clients who are not referred through the addict program. (This client is referred for the youth program.) The skills-training coordinator evidently asks if the client has any correctional background (which would qualify him for training under the crime prevention program). The counselor asks the client if he has ever been arrested or incarcerated. The client says no. The counselor asks the skills-training coordinator if there is any other way the client can qualify for training. Then he tells the client that the only possibility is through the crime prevention program, for "correctional clients." He hangs up the phone.

Counselor: But I will speak to D___ W___ [information service] about other training programs. But maybe you can get this stock job for now, while you're going to school at night.

The client indicates willingness to accept the stock job. The counselor discusses the client's work references (shown on a form filled out by the client). He gives the client advice on how to fill out an employment application correctly, such as putting the most recent job first.

Counselor: Employers judge applicants by whether they fill out the application correctly, and by the initial impression the employer forms of you.

The counselor tries to call the information service director. She is not at her desk. He asks the client if the agency's orientation program "explained the YEA services to you." The client says no. The counselor describes the agency and its services briefly.

Counselor: It is primarily a placement service. But we also do research and training. And the Information Service—which keeps up on the training programs available in the city. I also suggest you take a look at the *Occupational Outlook Handbook* [published by the Department of Labor] in the library. But now, I've got to get you a job. That's the main thing.

The counselor dials a phone number, trying to reach the employer who is hiring for the stock job. Wrong number. He dials again. No answer. He dials again—meanwhile asking the client if he has finished exams for this semester. Still no answer. He goes to the job development office to see if he has the right number. He returns, unable to find the job developer he was looking for. He calls his supervisor to see if the job developer is there. He is not there. The counselor sees another job developer walking by, and he asks him if *he* has the phone number. They go to the job development office to look it up. In a few minutes he returns and says he is having trouble getting the employer's number: "I don't think there will be any problem getting the job. I'm having someone check the number."

The job developer comes in and says the employer can't be reached. "He seems to be moving, [and is] probably in transit."

Counselor (to client): Just wait outside in the waiting room for a few minutes. I don't want you to leave while I have a job possibility for you.

The counselor and the client leave together. He returns shortly, and we talk briefly about the situation where training is limited to "correctionals." Then he goes to his supervisor's office, saying, "It's always an emergency with her!" He returns after about 10 minutes. "*She* took this [stock] job order!" he says. He dials Information to get the employer's phone number. The phone company has no new number.

Counselor: They [employer] are probably in transit. It is an old [long-time] employer.

The counselor calls another employer and asks if the packer jobs he listed a few days ago are still open. The employer asks about the OJT training subsidy. The counselor explains that it amounts to 50 percent of gross wages. The employer complains about the quality of the applicants sent thus far: They have little manual dexterity. The counselor says that future applicants can be tested for dexterity. The employer says he wants somebody who is "motivated." The counselor first verifies that the positions are still open, then says that applicants will be tested before being referred.

Counselor: Motivation is hard to check. But we will look at how long they worked on other jobs to gauge motivation.

The counselor interrupts his work for a minute to say something about his work with one particular client with whom he has been working since 1972. He was a problem case, always showing promise, but "always fucking up one way or another." The client is now married and a father (one child), and "earning $190 a week, as a spray painter. As long as I see motivation I will do everything I can." He adds: "I've gone fishing with him . . . . I reached him through sports . . . and I had him over to the house a few times."

Then he returns to his work. He dials the transit system to get travel directions to the stock job employer's (the first employer) place of business. The transit system information service has changed its number. He calls the new number and is put on "hold." He waits on the phone for a few minutes and then asks E__ M__ (job developer) to stay on the phone while he goes out to talk to the client. E___ M___ finally gets the travel directions. The counselor returns and makes arrangements to refer the client out for an interview, despite the fact that he has not yet contacted the employer. But he does not seem concerned about this: "He [employer] said just send the client out. They're just not picking up the phone."

While all this is going on, the counselor is trying to find a job for another client who is in the waiting room. This client now comes into the office with the counselor, who discusses the client's automotive driving experience. The client is expressive, confident in manner.

Client No. 2:   I want something I can stay in for a while, not something I will leave after a while. That's bad on my end and bad on your end.

The counselor explains the procedure for getting Police Department approval for tow-truck drivers (the type of job he has in mind for this client). It requires fingerprinting and takes time.

Counselor: Are you clean now on your [driving] record?
Client No. 2:   Oh, I'm clean. My license is clean.

The counselor calls an employer. This employer has no openings for tow-truck drivers now. The counselor asks the employer how long it takes to get a tow-truck license (about one month) and about the minimum age the employer will accept. The employer says he is now hiring only those in their late twenties because younger drivers have had too many accidents. The counselor hangs up the phone. He tells the client it shows how important a clean license is, because of insurance-rate problems for employers.

Counselor: I'll try another job. You know all parts of the city?
Client No. 2:   Yeah, I know all the parts.

The counselor leaves to get information about another job possibility. While he is away, the client says nothing; he looks down at the floor, at his cap; he twists his cap in his hands.

Counselor (returning):   I'll have to hold off on that job. But there is another possibility. A long shot. Can you get your license changed to a chauffeur's license?
Client No. 2:   I can go down to Motor Vehicles [department] today. But it will take at least two weeks. They will have to give me the chauffeur's road test. By that time, the job will be gone.   ·

The counselor leaves the office again, apparently to check out this last possibility. He returns in a few minutes.

Counselor: Good news! I have an appointment for you tomorrow morning. The job pays $4 an hour. But you will have to take their test—driving and written tests. I told them you had driving experience in the Army.

Client No. 2:   No problem! I'll take any test. I'll take my DD–214 [form, which summarizes the service record of veterans], my license and Social Security card. What's the job?

The client seems happy about this. He and the counselor leave the office together, the counselor filling him in further on the requirements of the job. It is now 12:30. The first client was seen at 10:30.

THE LOCAL JOB MARKET

The successful practice of vocational counseling, if it includes job placement, depends to a considerable extent on a favorable job market. For YEA's clientele, this would mean an abundance of entry-level jobs. In August 1974 YEA arranged a conference on assessment and goals for the purpose of determining what the agency should be doing in the future. One of the participants was a high regional official of the U.S. Department of Labor whose department monitored and issued the official reports on employment trends.

The Labor Department official reported that "since 1969, total non-agricultural employment has been on the decline in Center City, especially in manufacturing and wholesale retail trade," key areas through which young people had typically entered the job market. The official added that while 5 million new jobs had been created in the United States between 1971 and 1973, "Center City has remained in a recession and has lost approximately 250,000 jobs in the past four years," and that the city was "now into its fifth consecutive year of job loss." He observed that the "most alarming" aspect of this was the fact that the city was losing jobs "in what appears to be a geometric progression." Evidence for this was that in June 1974 the city had 41,000 fewer jobs than the year before, while in 1973 it had only 13,000 fewer jobs than in 1972.

The loss of jobs in the city was associated with an "astounding" rate of unemployment for minority-group teenagers. The total unemployment rate was said to be 5.8 percent. For white teenagers of both sexes the rate was "an unacceptable 15.3 percent." For low-income minority groups, the rates rose "drastically." The unemployment rates for these groups were:

Hispanic teenagers, female	30.1%
Black teenagers, female	32.7%
Black teenagers, male	35.8%
Hispanic teenagers, male	39.8%

Although there was some relief in sight for the city as a whole, based upon a projected growth in professional, technical and clerical occupations in certain industries, the situation for YEA's unskilled and uneducated clients would probably remain "dismal." The official concluded by saying that "the Center City labor market is increasingly being dominated by relatively low-paying white-collar type jobs that don't really present much potential opportunity or career development for the unskilled young male population now entering the workforce."

The outlook was indeed dismal, since a great many of the agency's clients (about 78 percent) were teenaged, minority-group males who experienced all the major "disabilities" cited: decline of entry-level jobs, low educational level, exclusion from clerical occupations, and so on. Moreover, as Center City lost jobs, competition for the remaining jobs became more intense. The projected "growth areas" (such as clerical, professional, and technical jobs) offered neither immediate nor future benefit. For one reason, those trends had not fully developed yet. When and if they did develop more fully, they were the kinds of jobs for which the agency's clients were only minimally qualified at best and the agency's present mode of operation was not designed to assist clients in preparation for such jobs.

The agency and its counselors had always been dependent on employers for disposal of their output, that is, placement of the clients. It was in the nature of the work. The counselors had developed techniques for "conning" employers and facilitating the placement of clients. For example, Counselor G reported that he let the employer lead the way in indicating which falsifications are required.

You start out with, "Have you ever dealt with our agency before? Or with any public or private agency?" These guys, the employers, come out with so much stuff—and you take it from there. Whatever their biases are, you try to explain that you're not like that. You know, he says, for example, "I'm getting rid of one person, and that person is deficient in a certain way." And I say, "Well, the person I have before me, the client, is not like that."

Counselor J reported that he too tells employers what they "want to hear." The difference is that all employers want to hear the same thing, in his judgment, namely, that the clients will be punctual and dependable. To this end he exaggerates or falsifies the agency's evaluative and preparatory procedures.

I always explain what the client goes through in our program. It's usually impressive to the employer. I tell him how we prepare clients—tell them about our Job Prep Program. I tell them how we measure punctuality: We have the kids come to us seven times before we send them on interviews. That we don't send them out on interviews just to see if they are punctual. And this, to an employer—that's what he wants to hear . . . . A lot of times, it's a snow job, because you're seeing the client for the first time. In this particular business, a lot of white-lying goes on because—like that salesman—you have to get that foot in the door first, to give the kid a chance to prove himself.

The efficacy of such techniques was limited, however, by job-market conditions, and even in the best of circumstances depended to some degree on employer good will. While unemployment for teenage minority-group members was never low, it grew worse under the influence of the recession and the changing structure of the city's labor market.

INTERNAL AND EXTERNAL OPPORTUNITIES

The hiring and training of counselors fostered dependence on the agency for employment. The counselors came with no professional credentials and left with none, when they did leave. Ironically, YEA had never encouraged counselors to believe that they could expect a career within the agency. The portrait itself as a low-cost agency required a frequent turnover of personnel so as to keep salaries and benefits to the minimum. The hiring of non-professional personnel also helped in this regard. When the agency began expanding in the mid-sixties, stimulated by the example of numerous anti-poverty agencies and by the seemingly inexhaustible supply of federal funds, there were abundant opportunities on the outside for counselors who found YEA's resources too limited, its philosophy too old-fashioned, or its salaries and promotional prospects too small. The agency was in effect a training ground for more affluent and more exciting agencies and for private companies and governmental agencies that offered greater rewards for the same kind of work.

By the mid-seventies, however, the picture had changed. Few private firms were hiring "minority-affairs" officials. The state employment service was laying off personnel. The "war on poverty" had virtually passed into history; fewer community-action agencies were left operating in Center City. Counselor G observed that formerly there were a "hundred community-action agencies begging for" the kind of experience obtained from working at YEA. Now, he added, that had changed. There were few opportunities available outside YEA. One effect of this change, it is suggested, was to bind the fate of the counselors even more closely to the fate of the agency—which had itself become more and more dependent on contract funding.

NOTES

1. We draw upon the work of three important writers in this area in our list of professional criteria. William J. Goode, "Community within a Community: The Professions" (*American Sociological Review*, April 1957), presents 11 criteria

of professional occupations. Some of these we have borrowed. However, we have chosen not to include the "service orientation" which he takes for granted; instead, we have discussed something of this kind under the heading of altruism. A. M. Carr-Saunders and P. A. Wilson, *The Professions* (New York: Oxford University Press, 1933), emphasize the professional's "prolonged intellectual training" and the resulting special techniques and attitudes. Here, we have de-emphasized the degree to which training is "prolonged" and have chosen instead to use "specialized training beyond the B.A. degree," since to strictly use Carr-Saunders' and Wilson's standards serves to limit consideration to medicine and law among what Friedson calls the "consulting professions." Eliot Freidson, *Profession of Medicine: A Study of the Sociology of Applied Knowledge* (New York: Dodd, Mead & Co., 1970), argues that the control over one's work (technical autonomy) is the principal distinguishing feature of a professional. However, we have not included this in our list of criteria partly because we have aimed at a consensus of opinion on this topic and partly because YEA's counselors seemed to possess considerable autonomy in their day-to-day work, as we report elsewhere. However, it is not so simple to consider them "professionals" for that reason. Friedson can conclude that technical autonomy is decisive when he discusses the medical profession, one that meets all the other standards we have proposed. YEA's counselors possess few of these other attributes, as we shall see. Thus, we would have to argue why they were professional in the sense of technical autonomy and *not* professional with respect to the other standards. We choose instead to discuss the findings under other headings such as the conflict over agency mission and organizational altruism, and to use here a more simple definition of "profession."

2. The American Personnel and Guidance Association (APGA) of which the National Vocational Guidance Association (NVGA) is a division, includes the second through the fifth of the items listed among the "marks of a profession" in its *Personnel and Guidance Standard Reference* (1973). The first area of specialization is taken for granted by APGA. As for the monopoly of jobs and limitation of training opportunities, there is, of course, no mention.

3. APGA *Personnel and Guidance Standard Reference*, p. 5.

4. For example, see C. Esco Obermann's article in the winter 1972–73 issue of *The Journal of Applied Rehabilitation Counseling*.

5. APGA *Personnel and Guidance Standards Reference*, p. 9.

6. We see in this case that it is not simply docility that the agency seeks, contrary to what may have been suggested by our earlier remarks about "control." It was observed that applicants for counseling positions who projected an image of "concern" (for the work, the clients, and so on) were often highly favored. Concern may have been gauged partly by the kind of work experience the applicant had and partly by the applicant's abilities in talking about the position. A good "salesman" had an advantage. Favored applicants were also seen to be "realistic" as well as "concerned."

4

Income and Contracts

For any organization, whether charitable or profit-making, the importance of money and the restrictions attached to it cannot easily be overestimated. Profit-makers may go into the capital market for unrestricted funds; bank loans, bond issues, and other sources are more restricted. For unrestricted funds charitable organizations go into their own capital market, under the guise of fund-raising. Funds obtained through contracts are more restrictive.

The source of YEA's income and the terms of the contract through which it was obtained played an important part in determining what the conselors did in practice, regardless of the expressed purpose of the contract; more than any other factor, the combination of income source and contract type influenced the changes in the agency during the period of research.

AGENCY INCOME

The agency's income came from four sources: (1) contributions from individuals, (2) grants from foundations, (3) corporate contributions, and (4) government contracts. The first three together represent the private money the agency received. Private money gives the agency considerable latitude in defining its mission and implementing it, compared with the more specific and limiting terms of government contracts. However, the growth of government programs in the manpower field in recent years had apparently caused potential contributors to look elsewhere for worthwhile charities. The shortage of private funds, combined with the agency's desire to expand its services, led it into the market for government contracts. Table 4.1 shows YEA's total budgets in recent years, the amounts and percentages of private and government funds each year, and the new programs that were added in that year. The trend of these figures can be seen at a glance in Figure 4.1.

Table 4.1
Private Funds and Total Income at YEA, 1964–1978

YEAR	Total Income	Private Funds	Govt. Funds	Private as % of Total	New Contracts Added
1964	$38,675	$28,592	$10,083	74	Juvenile Bureau (reform schools, etc.)
1967	143,106	28,012	115,094	19.6	On-the-job training (OJT)
1970	308,327	99,507	208,820	32	Jr. draftsman
1971	389,787	109,157	280,630	30	
1972	423,498	108,366	315,132	25	
1973	431,524	95,475	336,049	22	Ex-addict
1974	709,118	126,484	582,634	17.7	Crime prevention
1976	797,395	120,348	677,047	15	
1977	853,588	92,350	761,238	10.8	
1978	1,500,195	148,195	1,352,000	9.8	

There is no single turning point in the figures. The overall pattern is one of a gradual, increasing dependence on government contracts. The only exception to the otherwise consistent pattern is 1967 when the percentage of private took a precipitous drop due to the sudden injection of OJT funds. However, if there was a key period, it would seem to be the 1973–77 period. It was during this time, when two major new programs were inaugurated, that the gap between private and government funds became most pronounced. The percentage of private funds declined from 25 percent to about 10 percent, and the amount of government funds more than doubled: from around $315,000 to a little over $761,000.

By itself, the changing pattern of funding was significant but probably not all that decisive, even given the sizable gap between private and government funds beginning in 1973. The new factor introduced at that time, however, in combination with the funding pattern, did have a decisive effect on the agency. The new ingredient was a new (for YEA) type of contract with new terms of accountability.

Lipsky defines accountability as involving a relationship between people or groups that takes a patterned form: "One is always account-

Figure 4.1
Government Grants and Private Contributions, YEA, 1964–1977

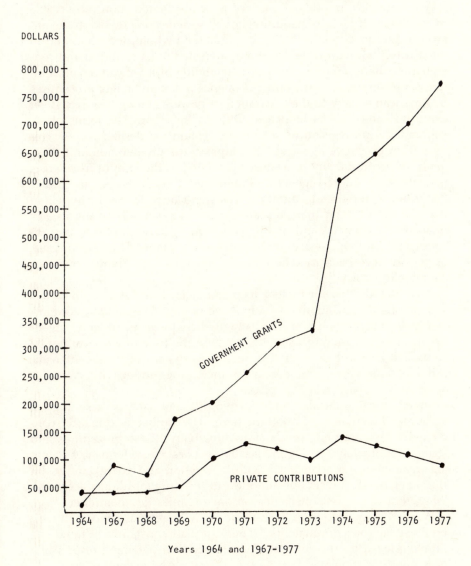

Years 1964 and 1967-1977

able *to* someone, never in the abstract . . . and only if a pattern of behavior exists can predictability, and therefore accountability, exist."[1]

Linder adds that accountability "refers to the enforcement of responsiveness through procedures that affect the value premises of administrators' decisions." Legislatures and courts, he observes, "rely upon

formal controls on administrative discretion to enforce responsiveness to certain values."[2]

Accountability is probably a very general phenomenon, observable in the major (if not all) institutions of all societies, expressed in the answer to the question, "Who is accountable to whom, for what, and in what way?" However, we are more interested in its historical and concrete form here, and whatever understanding of it we can obtain. Linder, for example, attributes the prevalence of accountability procedures in American society to the separation of powers among the legislative, executive, and judicial branches. Only by specifying the terms of accountability can legislatures and courts obtain the desired responsiveness from executive agencies.[3] For Lipsky, the proliferation and stringency of accountability procedures is related to the current fiscal crisis in state and federal agencies. Public agencies, he says, are under "enormous pressures to minimize costs and increase productivity" so that they can "claim that they are maintaining services in the face of financial stringency" and at the same time justify employee pay increases which they are also under pressure to grant.[4] The development of performance measures, he notes, is essential for a "bureaucratic accountability policy."[5]

Accountability is not limited to public agencies. But in both public and private organizations, we might see rational bureaucratic accountability as the contemporary and pragmatic equivalent of labor speedup and mechanization in situations where the pace of work cannot be controlled easily. Not since the early days of capitalism has intensification of labor been a major means of increasing productivity. Accountability has, in part, taken its place.

Lipsky and Linder also point to two different aspects or settings of accountability that are important here. The former is primarily concerned with intra-organizational accountability, those procedures and standards aimed at insuring predictable and desired performances within an organization in accordance with its mission and goals. Linder, on the other hand, directs our attention to inter-organizational accountability, that is, the responsiveness of one organization to another.

Weber's classic work on bureaucracy may be seen as concerned with both aspects of accountability.[6] There he had constantly in mind the problem faced by the ruler or elected official of obtaining responsiveness from the appointed bureaucratic officials. And in the earliest stages of development, collegiate bodies and later bureaucracies were depicted by Weber as monarchic innovations in the face of independent (thus non-accountable) nobilities and parliaments. In this sense, Weber dealt with the inter-organizational aspect of bureaucracy. For the most part, however, this essay was devoted to the internal workings of bureaucracy: the hierarchical structure, official duties, salaried compensation, general rules, and impersonal relations that chained the bureaucrat to his job and helped ensure his compliance with the directives of superiors.

The general rules, official duties, and impersonal relations would all seem to require the development of objective standards of performance. Weber does not discuss this explicitly in the essay on bureaucracy, but elsewhere notes the importance in a money economy of numerical measures of performance.[7] The rationality of money accounting has as one primary consequence the formulation of numerical statements "of (a) the prospects of every projected course of economic action, and (b) assessment of the results of every completed action." In the bureaucracy essay, Weber argues that a money economy is one of the presuppositions of bureaucracy. Not only does a money economy provide the means for regular salaried compensation for officials but it appears to inject its fundamental numerical rationality into this bureaucracy.

Although Weber's work is focused on the intra-organizational features of bureaucracy (and thus accountability), it is nevertheless applicable to our analysis of the events observed at YEA. This is so, but not because YEA had itself become highly bureaucratic. (It had not, although there were certain tendencies in the direction.) Rather, it seems that under conditions of dependence on large bureaucratic government agencies, bureaucratic premises and standards come to be more important in the dependent organization. What was external becomes internal. Perhaps we can see this more clearly by first taking a closer look at the Comprehensive Employment and Training Act (CETA) and then briefly examining YEA's contracts.

ACCOUNTABILITY IN CETA

The CETA program along with certain other legislative accomplishments of the early seventies such as revenue-sharing and the Professional Standards Review Organization (PSRO) represented a convergence of the political right and left in terms of a demand for greater accountability from both private and public institutions. The proliferation of manpower programs in the sixties and their location in different agencies precluded effective accountability for manpower policy. Divided responsibility and diverse practices presented an untidy and unwieldy spectacle to those concerned with this important area of policy. Mirengoff and Rindler observe that one of the major expectations for CETA was that "the jumble of categorical programs would be transformed into an orderly array of program activities in each community."[8] Davidson says that coordination among the major federal agencies—including the Department of Labor (DOL), Department of Health,

Education, and Welfare (HEW), and the Office of Economic Opportunity (OEO)—competing for preeminence in the manpower field was frequently discussed in the 1960s but little was done.[9] The fragmentation of the manpower effort was "a product not only of agency rivalries," he argues, "but also, and more fundamentally, of the manner in which policies are formulated and sustained in a pluralist political system"; each new and pressing need identified by the legislature led to "a mosaic of single-purpose efforts, with inevitable discord" when incorporated into legislation.[10]

Thus, one common ground for those concerned with manpower policy was "rationalization," or consolidation of the overlapping programs so as to obtain greater coordination of efforts and more clearly fixed responsibility. Under these conditions, Mirengoff and Rindler note, local delivery agencies would be able to "become more efficient and effective."[11] In Davidson's view, one of the major drawbacks of the uncoordinated array of programs developed during the sixties was that both operating agencies and consumers found it confusing and difficult to obtain manpower funds or services because each federal agency had its own unique standards and funded separate facilities.[12] What was needed was one comprehensive manpower program.

Although some rationalization of the manpower program was needed, this did not include centralized administration and standardized programs. On the contrary, decentralization and programs tailored to local needs (decategorization) were consistent themes in the major legislative proposals that preceded CETA and in CETA itself. Decentralization and decategorization were the other common grounds of the new accountability that are of interest here.

Mirengoff and Rindler note that with the passage of CETA, "program control shifted from the federal level to more than 400 state and local units of government": Cities and consortia of smaller towns and counties were to run their own manpower programs, with the state governments responsible for the remainder of the state. Programs lost their separate categorical identities and funding. These changes were expected to permit greater flexibility in fashioning programs to local circumstances, the authors say; they further note the divergent groups satisfied by the program:

This reform of the manpower system appealed to pragmatic administrators seeking a more rational way to conduct employment and training activities, to those attracted by the features of grass roots participation, and to those committed to a reduction of the federal role"[13]

CETA contained five principal sections. Title I authorized comprehensive manpower services for the unemployed, underemployed, and economically disadvantaged. Programs were to be designed and administered by "prime sponsors," which were cities and counties with populations of 100,000 or more and consortia of smaller units, with the state government being the prime sponsor for the "balance of state." As with all decentralized titles, prime sponsors must submit acceptable plans to the secretary of labor. Title II provided funds to local prime sponsors and Indian reservations, in areas of substantial unemployment, to hire the unemployed for public-service jobs. Title III consolidated some of the existing nationally administered programs for Indians, migrant workers, youth, and other groups that might be identified. Title IV authorized continuation of the Job Corps by the Federal Department of Labor. Title IV was similar to Title II in that it authorized the creation of public-service jobs in areas of high unemployment. Unlike Title II, however, which was intended to offer temporary aid, Title IV was meant to be a permanent program (if needed), with aid triggered by the number of unemployed and an unemployment rate in excess of 4.5 percent.

CETA contained a mixture of categorical and non-categorical programs aimed at structural as well as cyclical unemployment, with some being administered nationally and some being decentralized. Categorical programs are those restricted to a particular category of persons, such as youth. Structural unemployment refers to the persistent exclusion of some groups from the labor market (for example, minority groups or those with little education), while cyclical unemployment refers to economic downturns that affect larger portions of the labor force. With respect to these features, the titles of CETA can be summarized in the following table.

	Aimed at Structural Unemployment	Aimed at Cyclical Unemployment
Categorical and Centralized	Title III Title IV	
Non-categorical and Decentralized	Title I	Title II Title IV

Mirengoff and Rindler comment that, by 1978 the "first and central strategic objective of CETA, decentralization," had been achieved.[14] To a point, the assertion was true: Local units of government were designing and administering their own manpower program presumably based on local needs. This applied especially to Title I programs for the disadvantaged, and it was this title that was the principal source of funds obtained by YEA. Looked at in other ways, however, the judgment regarding decentralization is open to question. The political decentralization achieved was deceptive as long as determination of the premises and the standards of locally originated programs remained in Washington.

Although claiming that decentralization had been achieved, Mirengoff and Rindler note that there had been no abdication of federal oversight responsibilities and that the degree of "federal presence" continued to be a thorny issue. While 90 percent of the fiscal 1978 CETA funds were said to be in programs under local control, increasing federal constraints on programs could be seen—constraints arising from an emphasis on DOL accountability, which limited local autonomy.[15]

The same authors note that in their study, 15 of the 18 prime sponsors in the sample reported increased contact with regional DOL officials in the previous year. Monitoring and assessment activities, along with grant modifications (some due to funding changes), were said to be the reasons for most contacts.[16] The prime sponsors appeared to evaluate their local program operators in the same way, that is, in the more narrow terms of contract compliance rather than in any broader context—as a device for comparing different service strategies, comparing how effective the programs were on various target groups, or studying how the program as a whole related to the objectives of the overall manpower programs.[17]

The authors recognize the differences that existed regarding the merits of a structured, quantitative approach to monitoring. Prime sponsors and DOL officials were said to favor it because they believed it would help reduce costs, lead to better performance, and help identify weak areas. However, critics, especially those actually operating manpower programs, contended that the structural approach put too much emphasis on placement; thus, it directed services to those applicants with the best chances for placement, discouraged the use of more comprehensive services and long-range programs, and in general tended to impose uniform standards on programs, many of which had unique characteristics such as the qualifications of clients and local labor market conditions.[18]

YEA'S CONTRACTS

Levitan and Taggart have commented that in manpower programs, perhaps more than in any other area, emphasis has been placed on "measuring and evaluating performance, comparing alternative approaches, and making decisions based on hard evidence rather than exhortation," despite the fact that the experimental method, their measures, and their impact have not been extensively analyzed.[19] We might apply the substance of these remarks to manpower contracts also.

Earlier we considered the ratio of private funds to contract funds under the heading of organizational dependence. Here, we look at the problem in terms of contract types. Funds that the agency receives can be classified with respect to the power of the definitions they impose upon the agency, and consequently with respect to the agency's "room to maneuver" in meeting the requirements imposed. The types of funding, in order of the freedom allowed to the agency, are:

Type of Funding	*Example*
1. Private money	Funds raised by chairman
2. Best-effort contracts	Delinquency program
3. Performance contracts	Addict program
4. Purchase-of-services contracts	Crime-prevention program

Private money has no conditions or requirements attached to it. This includes the money raised by the chairman with his annual fund-raising letter, and foundation grants for "general purposes." As we saw earlier, this kind of money now represents a very small part of the agency's annual income.

Best-effort contracts are those that specify a minimum number of clients to be seen and accepted for service. The agency is required to make its best effort in placing the clients on jobs but there are no specific requirements. These contracts are apparently a thing of the past. The delinquency program, an example of this type, was not renewed by the state in 1975. The youth program, formerly a "best-effort contract," is now a "performance contract" since the allocation of government funds was centralized in one city department and funding organizations have grown more knowledgeable about the work of placement.

Performance contracts are those that specify (1) *goals,* such as job placement and retention and skills-training quotas; (2) *tasks,* such as registration, orientation, counseling, follow-up, and teaching; (3) *resources,* such as videotape equipment, specialized personnel, skills-training allowances, and stipends; and (4) *penalties* for failure to perform according to standard. These contracts include funds for specified positions at specified salaries, plus allocations for specific equipment and anticipated costs (phone bills, for example).

Purchase-of-services contracts pay only upon delivery of specified services, such as placement on a job and retention on a job for specified periods. No positions are directly funded. No specific equipment or other expenses are covered. All the necessary costs of placing and keeping clients on jobs are supposedly included in the per capita fees.

Performance and purchase-of-services contracts are, for YEA, the most important of these types at the present time.

PERFORMANCE CONTRACTS: THE ADDICT PROGRAM

An example of a contract of this type is the one between Center City's Department of Employment and the Youth Employment Agency. The value of the contract at the time was $210,361. This amount included stipends and tuition for skills-training. The contract funded the equivalent of 12 positions:

1 Skills-training and project manager

1 bookkeeper

3 Placement counselors

3 Post-placement counselors

1 Remedial-education instructor

1 Clerk

1 Job developer

$^{1}/_{2}$ of the psychometrician's salary

$^{1}/_{4}$ of the associate director's salary

$^{1}/_{4}$ of the fiscal administrator's salary

The contract required YEA to "operate and administer a manpower services project to provide services as defined below to 488 unemployed or underemployed rehabilitated drug addicts in Center City."

The official referral sources are designated, as are the criteria for client acceptability. The services (or tasks) are specified as intake, orientation, counseling, testing, job preparation, referral to job, remediation, and vocational training. Some tasks, such as referral, are spelled out in some detail. For example, YEA was required to "offer each person accepted for manpower services at least three job referrals." And if an enrollee did not report for a scheduled interview with the employer or was not hired, the contract stated that the agency "shall make every effort to contact the client and make another appropriate referral."

As for minimum placement and retention requirements, YEA agreed to place at least 256 enrollees (52 percent of the minimum 488 enrollees), with at least 50 percent of them being retained by the employer for at least 30 consecutive working days. The retention requirement could be met on "either the first placement or any subsequent placement."

YEA would fail to perform satisfactorily if it fell "substantially below the minimum placement levels set forth" in the contract, or if its unit costs for placement and retention exceeded the allowable limits. In these cases, the contract budget could be "adjusted," that is, reduced. YEA was also required to allow the funding agency "full access to the contractor's accounts, books, records and any other information relative to the operation of the project . . . . "

The funding agency assigned a program monitor to examine the reports and keep track of the performance schedule month by month. Deficiencies such as falling behind in placements were noted in the monitor's monthly evaluation (submitted to his superiors and ultimately to YEA). The monitor also went to YEA's office each month, armed with the list of individuals claimed as placements by YEA, for the purpose of verifying placements. This was done by selecting a few names at random from the list and having a counselor call the employer to verify that the client was still working while (unknown to the employer) the monitor listened in on the conversation.

A PURCHASE-OF-SERVICES CONTRACT: THE CRIME-PREVENTION PROGRAM

This contract was funded by the city's Joint Council for Crime Prevention, which was set up to coordinate programs of this type using city, state, and federal funds. A total of $140,800 was available to YEA. However, to obtain the funds YEA had to make verified placements and verified retentions for specified periods. There was a "projected staffing" of two intake and evaluation counselors, two post-placement counselors, and two clerk-bookkeepers. No positions, as such, were directly funded, although the agency's table of organization showed that one intake counselor, one post-placement counselor, and one clerk were assigned to the program. "Skills-training" and "remedial education" were included among the services to be provided but did not involve the assignment of personnel. Rather, clients in this program were to have access to these services. "Skills-training placements" in public and private training facilities were rewarded by a fee. Remedial education, however, was not compensated; educationally handicapped clients were to be serviced by YEA's remedial-education program. In general, income was based on results: job placements and retentions and enrollment in vocational-training facilities.

The services performed were "vouchered" each month: A claim for payment was submitted, with the services classified and enumerated. The fees were supposed to cover the costs of servicing approximately 250 clients by providing (1) pre-employment orientation and counseling, (2) remedial instruction as needed, (3) placement into approved vocational skills-training programs where appropriate, and (4) post-placement counseling. The contract provided money for specific purposes, in contrast to funding specific staff positions. These budgeted amounts included the following:

Purpose	Amount in Budget
Client stipends	$37,800
Vocational training (tuition)	20,000
Client travel	1,000
Staff travel	500
Initial job placement	55,000
Subsequent job placement	5,000
Remedial education	18,200
Supplies	3,300

Stipends of up to $50 per week were available to clients who needed financial assistance to seek employment. Preference was given to those who were "unemployed and enrolled in remedial or skills training programs."

When the agency made a placement or achieved a retention or enrolled a client in an approved skills-training program, it billed the funding organization for payment in accordance with the schedule of payments set forth in the contract. For example, for an initial job placement YEA was paid $60 for each day the client was employed, to a maximum of $300. For subsequent job placements, the payment was $100 each, with two such placements being allowed. For each month the client worked on a given job, the agency got $55, to a maximum of $330. And for each client enrolled in an approved vocational-training program the agency received $150. In this program, YEA was required to place a client on "one subsequent job if he or she loses the first job for whatever reason"—unlike the addict program, which required "three referrals" but no subsequent placement.

The responsibilities of the post-placement counselors were enumerated: They were to be responsible for "ongoing personal assistance to all employed clients, including counseling on job-related problems, personal financing advice, and development of long-range career goals."

The implications of YEA's dependence on government contracts were not lost on the staff. In 1972, one of the agency's contracts was not renewed. This contract was for counseling and placement services for youth released from the city's prison. The director notified the executive committee of the board in a memo on March 27. The memo noted that the contract was canceled for "lack of performance." Only 132 clients had been serviced instead of the required 300. For these 132 clients 83 placements were achieved. The funding agency claimed that "despite the lack of clients, a better quality and more placements and higher retention rate might have been expected," and that "the number of placements did not justify the $50,000 spent." The director's memo then listed the staff positions that were jeopardized by loss of the contract. These positions included a vocational counselor, a placement counselor, a job developer, and a clerk. The director noted that YEA's president had given instructions "to reduce staff accordingly."

The lost contract had further ramifications: It was funded by the same city agency that funded another of YEA's programs. When the executive staff had met on March 24, the director pointed out that "the chances are that this contract will not be renewed also." "Our only hope is the Juvenile Bureau contract," he said. The director ordered that "every one of these clients must be placed unless there is documented proof that they cannot be placed for reasons beyond our control" and added that clients in the youth program and those from the Juvenile Bureau would "have preference over non-contract clients."

The remainder of the March 24 meeting was spent in deciding who should be laid off and when, and in a reassignment of duties of some staff members and supervisors. Agency personnel were told about the impending layoff in a staff meeting held a few days later, although the individuals to be laid off were not identified. Two of the staff members identified in the memo were in fact let go: one counselor and one job developer. The agency used the cancellation to "get rid of dead wood" since the counselor released had not been assigned to the contract. Those who remained were absorbed into other services, although in some cases they had to be paid out of agency rather than contract funds.

Two additional contracts were lost during the period of study. One of them (the addict program) was a sizable one, straining the agency's ability to absorb displaced workers. In fact, they could not be absorbed entirely. But some of the "dead wood" was quickly replaced by new workers. The other contract lost was the Juvenile Bureau contract—the delinquency program—which previously had been renewed every year since its inception. The Juvenile Bureau contract did not cause problems of the same magnitude as did the others, primarily because arrangements were made to accept Juvenile Bureau clients under the crime-prevention program. Thus, the staff members affected were able to be reassigned.

Administrators and supervisors anticipated possible layoffs when contracts were in trouble. In 1976 the addict program was running behind schedule. The supervisor of the program acted quickly in an attempt to bring the placements up so as to save the contract and to protect himself and his staff from blame. Minutes of the April 1, 1976 meeting of the addict program staff show that the supervisor described the situation to his subordinates in the following terms:

With only three months remaining to the Addict Program contract, it is noted that placements are down almost 50 %. Strong measures must be taken to at-

tempt to save the contract, so that the agency does not default on its obligations. The Director will state that he increased the number of job development
staff members, and therefore, the default of the contract now falls upon the
Addict Program staff. Therefore, the following guidelines are effective immediately. Any person not adhering to the following set of rules will receive one
note of warning. If this note does not change the situation, that person will
then be fired; no questions asked. This warning is final!

Although the counselors themselves had no placement quotas, they
were fully aware that the agency lived and died by placements—and to
a lesser degree, though increasingly important, by retentions. Excerpts
from a few of the interviews bearing on this point follow. For example,
when asked if the counselor's ability to establish rapport with clients
should be used in evaluating counselors, Counselor H replied, only "if
this was a different kind of agency. The bottom line here is placements." Another said that "the counselor has to push out a lot of prod-
ucts and cannot put out his best effort," and still another said that
"qualitative work is really needed." The same theme was repeated by
two other counselors, one of whom said that at YEA there was "not
enough emphasis on quality work" and too much emphasis on the
"numbers game."

Observations of the counselors at work also showed the effects of these
pressures. Compared with the earlier, more leisurely pace of work, the
counselors' work acquired a much more businesslike and purposeful
tone, with efforts directed toward quick placement. The counselors attempted to induce or persuade clients to accept jobs that were available
at the moment. As a general rule, they repeatedly directed a client's
attention from jobs desired by the client to a consideration of the ad-
vantages of a job that was open at the time or one that could easily be
procured.

Only one person (Counselor J) saw placement of the client as being
useful in facilitating the kind of counseling that many counselors said
they desired to do. This counselor said, "It's easier for him to think
with a straight head when there's money coming in . . . a person is
more rational . . . . And then you get into the other areas [of personal
problems] slowly."

Counselor G was asked if there should be a placement quota for
counselors. "Yeah, definitely," he responded. "There are people in the
field interested in *qualitative* things. Just what these qualitative things
are, nobody has been really able to define. Or, once defined, not everybody has been able to agree on which ones to use." The same counselor did note, however, that there is a time when "these qualitative
things have to be used." And he remarked, "You just can't forget that

these kids are 16 or 17 years old. That they are still not mature enough to want a steady job."

Regardless of the client's maturity, however, the contracts increasingly (and insistently) called for placement in a steady job. YEA was in a position where it had to comply, in one way or another.

NOTES

1. Michael Lipsky, "The Assault on Human Services: Street-Level Bureaucrats, Accountability, and the Fiscal Crisis," in Scott Greer et al. (eds.), *Accountability in Urban Society: Public Agencies under Fire* (Beverly Hills: Sage Publications, 1978), p. 15.

2. Stephen H. Linder, "Administrative Accountability: Administrative Discretion, Accountability, and External Controls," in Greer et al., p. 181.

3. Ibid.

4. Ibid., p. 27.

5. Ibid., p. 23.

6. Max Weber, "Bureaucracy," in *From Max Weber: Essays in Sociology* eds. Hans Gerth and C. Wright Mills (New York: Oxford University Press, 1946).

7. See, for example, Talcott Parsons (ed.), *Max Weber: The Theory of Social and Economic Organization* (New York: Free Press, 1964; originally published by Oxford University Press, 1947)., p. 186.

8. William Mirengoff and Lester Rindler, *CETA: Manpower Programs under Local Control* (Washington, D.C.: National Academy of Sciences, 1978), p. 137.

9. Roger H. Davidson, *The Politics of Comprehensive Manpower Legislation* (Baltimore: Johns Hopkins University Press, 1972), p. 5.

10. Ibid., p. 7.

11. See Mirengoff and Rindler, p. 137.

12. See Davidson, pp. 8–9.

13. See Mirengoff and Rindler, p. 2.

14. Ibid., p. 3.

15. Ibid. Emphasis added.

16. Ibid., p. 89.

17. Ibid., p. 108.

18. Ibid., p. 109.

19. Sar A. Levitan and Robert Taggart III, *Social Experimentation and Manpower Policy: The Rhetoric and the Reality* (Baltimore: Johns Hopkins University Press, 1971), p. 2.

5

Contract Compliance: The Statistical Reports

Statistical reports, for an agency such as YEA, are a product—a commodity—and like any commodity should be carefully crafted. Although it is a service agency, the services are not exchanged with the contractor. The quality of the services—even their actual delivery—is largely unknown to the funding agency. Between YEA and the funding agency there is an exchange of money for statistical reports.

Keeping in mind YEA's growing dependence on contracts and the detailed terms of accountability spelled out in the contracts, two things might be expected: (1) Tasks other than those required will be ignored, and (2) the statistical reports required will be crafted, whenever possible, to be favorable to the agency. The tasks are covered in a later chapter. As for the statistical reports, the topic of this chapter, we are interested mainly in just how favorable reports were constructed, since it will not surprise anyone that this was done.

Stanton describes the process of "concealment" of reality in the mental health field. Mental health agencies, she said, "distort information in meeting the United Fund requirements for quantifiable public relations data." The number of people served by these agencies is arbitrarily defined as "all the patients in all the mental hospitals, all the people who request booklets, all the volunteers who are provided educational experiences by participating in the work of the Association (including those who contribute to the Christmas campaign), and all the people in the audiences at Association functions or at meetings addressed by a member of the Speakers Bureau." Stanton observed that the total is "an impressive public relations figure."[1]

The mental health agency that Stanton described attempted to define success in terms of how many people were contacted in any way. These people were, by the agency's definition, "served." The Youth Employment Agency used similar bases for defining success: number of clients seen, number of interviews held, number of referrals, and so on. The most important one, however, was placements. Whenever possible (and even the new programs had trouble policing this), the administrators claimed success on the basis of total placements (including multiple placements for the same client) rather than the placement of a given number of clients. Where this produced impossible results (more placements than clients accepted for a program), success was claimed in terms of an *increase in placements* over the previous year, or the comparable period in the previous year, or the previous period in the same year. Only when no basis for success could be found, which occasionally happened, were the reasons for failure carefully documented.[2]

Since YEA's purpose was to help individuals in certain specific ways aimed at placing them on jobs, the number of total placements would not seem to be an appropriate measure because it included multiple placements for the same individual. More than that, the agency's statistics included placements on "day jobs" such as temporary messenger and delivery jobs. Some of these may have been converted into permanent jobs if the employer was satisfied with the work of the employee, but most were not.

The agency had no knowledge of the number of individuals placed on permanent jobs. But administrators have reported to contract agencies that as many as 78 percent of the clients were placed. This figure was derived by comparing the number of clients seen with the number of total placements made by the agency. The number of placements, as noted, includes multiple placement and day jobs.

This measure of success was not inconsistent with the reporting procedures of the "best-effort contracts." Such contracts usually called for registering and attempting to place a given number of clients. However, there were no reporting requirements based on the number of individuals actually placed, even though the wording of the contracts indicated that the funding agencies were primarily interested in the placement of as many individuals as possible, and not the total number of placements achieved by the agency.

For the period November 1, 1972, through June 30, 1973, the agency's performance is shown in Table 5.1. The figures were obtained from

Table 5.1
Agency Placements, November 1972–June 1973

	Number	Percentage
Clients seen	2,008	100
Placements recorded	1,045	52
Individuals placed	670	33

the associate director at the request of the investigator. The number of individuals placed includes those placed in temporary or day jobs. The associate director was reluctant to separate those out.[3]

We can, however, gain some idea of how many of the 670 individuals placed were placed on temporary jobs. The daily sheets for the month of May 1972 and October 1972 were analyzed for the ratio of temporary placements to all placements. Of the 171 placements made in May 1972, 47 percent were on temporary jobs. Of the 163 placements recorded in October 1972, 47 percent were on temporary jobs. Using this percentage we can estimate that of the 670 individuals placed in the November 1972–June 1973 period, 355 were placed on permanent jobs (out of the 2,008 clients seen)—a placement rate of 17.6 percent.[4]

This does not appear to be an impressive performance and would hardly satisfy any contract. We need not judge the performance, especially since the difficulty of the work is granted, but we should note that apart from this exceptional incident the agency did not know what its actual performance was. The administrators, we might conjecture, did not want to know because they would then have had to deliberately conceal or falsify the agency's performance. As it is, they did not have to do so because they did not know the truth.[5]

A more direct test of the agency's placement rate was made in a later stage of the research. In 1976 a sample of client records was selected from both the active files and the most recently inactivated files. The latter are files on clients who had not been serviced by the agency in two years. These records were "retired," or inactivated, in July 1975; thus the clients had not been serviced by the agency since at least June 1973. Applicants for part-time and summer jobs were excluded from the sample. Part-time jobs that fit a student's school hours are extremely hard to find, and thus failure would be almost certain. Summer applicants faced a similar situation, resulting from the large surplus of summer-job applicants from all over the city, and in addition they did not well represent the regular YEA clientele, since they were not dropouts. After eliminating the part-time and summer applicants from the sample, 168 cases remained: 79 from the inactive files and 89 from the active files.

The definition of "success" in this analysis was placement of an individual on at least one full-time permanent job within the first year of service. The "first year of service" criterion is necessary because clients did not all come to the agency at the same time. To compare the sample with the agency's reported placement rates—which were based on activity for a given one-year period—it is necessary to establish a comparable time period. The placement figures presented here are not *directly* comparable with any agency reports, however. To do that would have required selecting a sample from among the clients seen during any one reporting year. This could have been done, though it would have been a more time-consuming task. However, the procedure followed does allow a comparison with some of the agency's reports, and at the same time, we can observe how many placements the agency would claim from the sample. Table 5.2 shows how many placements were achieved by the operational definition, the placement rate or percentage for the entire sample of client files, and the number of placements the agency would claim.

For the same activity with the same group of clients, the agency would claim almost three times as many placements as could be claimed by the stricter definition of placement success proposed here. We might note that placement is affected by several factors, other than the motivation of clients previously discussed. Three factors were observed to be associated with placement rates: sex, age, and source of referral (or "program").

In the sample cases, 33 percent of the males were placed in full-time permanent jobs, while only 23 percent of the females were placed. Younger clients (16–19 years of age) were placed less frequently than older ones (20 and over); the percentages were 27 percent and 39 percent, respectively. When age and sex were combined, the older male clients were the most placeable group, and the older female clients were the least placeable: 44 percent of the former (19 out of 43) were placed on full-time jobs, compared with 11 percent (1 out of 9) of the latter. The placement rate for younger clients was the same for both sexes: about 26 percent. There were also some differences observed when we compared clients according to which program they were referred to (or, conversely, from which external agency they were referred). The nature of the program and its clientele—whether addicts, probationers, or some other special group—probably had something to do with the placeability of the clients, as did the referral agency's work in screening and preparing clients for YEA. Although the number of cases was small when the sample was sorted out in this way, the results showed that only 6 percent (1 out of 15) crime-prevention program clients were placed

Table 5.2
Individuals Placed in Full-time Permanent Jobs in First Year (Compared with Total Placements for First Year of Service)

Sample size	168
Full-time (F/T) placements	51
Placement rate	30%
Total placements claimed by agency	141

in full-time permanent jobs. By contrast, 67 percent (8 out of 12) of the addict program clients were placed. The showing for the former group was undoubtedly affected by the fact that those clients more often did not return to YEA after the first interview: Seven out of the 15 (46 percent) did not return, while only two out of the 12 (17 percent) addict clients failed to return.

TRADITION AND TOTAL PLACEMENTS

The claim for success based on total placements did not begin with the best-effort contracts, nor did it originate with the present associate director. The minutes of the January 14, 1942, meeting of the agency's board of directors show that the staff reported its success for December 1941 in terms of "number of boys handled" and "number of jobs obtained" (placements). At that time the agency handled only males. There was no indication of how many jobs obtained were multiple placements for the same client.

TOTAL PLACEMENTS, DECEMBER 1941

	Boys Handled	Jobs Obtained
White	53	29 (55%)
Black	50	30 (60%)
Total	103	59 (57%)

However, we can see more clearly the early use of total placement figures in the agency's report to the board for the period of February 1–August 21, 1947. This report was quite detailed, giving the name and home address of every client seen during the period, the date of registration at the agency, the referring agency, the date of placement, name and address of the employer, the job in which the client was placed, and the salary or wage rate.[6] The summary at the end of the report showed total placements by number and percentage. Note that by then, females were also accepted.

SUMMARY: TOTAL PLACEMENTS, FEBRUARY 1-AUGUST 21, 1947

Boys	Number	Percentage
Total Applicants	137	100
Total Placements	82	60
Girls		
Total Applicants	67	100
Total Placements	26	39

	Number	*Percentage*
Total Number of Applicants	204	100
Total Number of Placements	108	53

The "total number of placements" did not mean "number of clients placed," however. This was verified by counting the number of clients placed at least one time. The analysis showed that 97 (rather than 108) clients were placed at least once; of these, 87 were placed on one job, nine were placed on two jobs, and one was placed on three jobs—a total of 108 placements.[7] At that time, however, there were no contractual requirements for more precise figures. The staff reported only to the board which, for its own reasons, may have been inclined to accept the somewhat inflated figures.

TRADITION AND NEW REQUIREMENTS

The contract agencies are more precise in their demands than the board of directors had been. The addict program contract, for example, stated that "the Contractor agrees to place at least 256 enrollees." Enrollees, we recall, are clients who are accepted into the program on the basis of meeting the standards imposed by YEA. The 256 enrollees who were to be placed represent 52 percent of the 488 enrollees who were to be accepted under the contract. These terms clearly do not envision program success in terms of "placement activity." Enrollees are distinct individuals, not placements. The crucial measure for YEA was the *number* of unduplicated placements with a 30-day retention period. A total of 256 enrollees were to be placed on jobs (with half of them staying on the job for at least 30 working days).

The report submitted to the funding agency, Narcotic Rehabilitation Agency (NRA), after the first year of the program also reported the total placements achieved, rather than the number of enrollees placed. This report showed the following activities (among many others) for the year:

Appointments for initial screening	1156
Appointments kept	681
Appointments not kept	475
Number of placements	384
Clients accepted into skills training program	81
Clients reporting for skills training program	68

The 681 "appointments kept" appear to represent the number of enrollees in the program. If 384 of them were placed, the placement rate would be 56 percent—quite creditable. This appearance is strengthened

on page 8 of the report. Under the heading of "Follow-up and Retention Statistics" it is claimed that "384 *clients* were placed on jobs" (emphasis added). However, a footnote on page 1 says that of the 681 clients
who kept their initial appointments, "245 of these clients were rejected
by YEA." This seems to mean that only 436 enrollees were accepted
into the program. If there were 384 *individuals* placed out of this number, the placement rate would be 88 percent, not an easy achievement
with any group, let alone such a "disadvantaged" one. The result is
that we simply cannot tell what the performance was on this contract,
either in terms of a placement rate (as defined here) or in terms of individuals placed. The funding agency was in the same position. Apparently it never found out how many enrollees were placed. Relying
on its monitoring system, involving phone calls to the employers of only
a sample of reported placements, the NRA did not check for multiple
placements. YEA could not credibly claim the placement rate of 88 percent implicit in its statistics, and did not do so. But it did manage to
create the impression of placing 384 enrollees, thus surpassing the quota
of 256.

ALTERNATIVE IMAGES OF SUCCESS

The use of total-placement figures was not the only means of pro-
jecting an image of success employed by the agency. Other means of
accomplishing the same thing included claiming success on peripheral
tasks, the exploitation of loopholes, and the negotiation of favorable
definitions in contracts at the outset.

The report to the funding agency cited above (NRA) did not need to
claim success based on peripheral tasks, since the appearance of success was established (and apparently acknowledged by NRA) based on
placements. Nevertheless, success in several peripheral tasks was
claimed—perhaps as insurance. These included (1) number of jobs developed (2,373); (2) range of jobs in which enrollees were placed (a list
of 76 different jobs was included); (3) a study of the reasons for rejecting clients; and (4) a study of why clients lost or quit their jobs. In other
programs, by accepting more than the required number of enrollees,
by making psychometric evaluations (if not funded), or by doing any
other service not required in the contract, the agency could advance an
additional claim for success—and did so, especially if success in placements was lacking.

"Double-counting" is one form of exploiting loopholes in order to show
success. This involved, for example, referring an addict program client
to the on-the-job training (OJT) program. The latter subsidized employment and training in private firms. When the client was hired by an
"OJT employer," both the OJT and the addict programs claimed a

placement. This was justified by the director because both OJT and the addict program had had to service the client, one to assess the client and make the decision to refer him, and the other to place him. Double-counting was useful for all funded programs. Some evidence of this can be seen in the OJT placements reported for March 1976. Of the 48 clients placed that month by the OJT staff, only nine were referred to YEA by non-contract agencies. The remaining 39 placements were credited to both OJT and one of the three other contract programs within YEA, either the addict or the youth or the crime-prevention program. However, this did not solve the problem of placement for the other programs: OJT accepted only the better-than-average clients from them.[8]

Finally, the negotiation of favorable definitions grew more important to YEA as its contracts came to include more specific standards of performance. If the contract called for placement of a certain number of enrollees, the agency could and did try to make sure that the clients it accepted (its enrollees) were "placeable" so as not to waste time on more marginal clients. For example, the negotiated criteria for rejecting would-be enrollees in the addict program included the following:

1. Severe educational deficiencies, such as reading below the 5th grade level
2. Serious lack of motivation
3. Evidence of narcotics use
4. Failure to keep appointments, or repeated lateness for appointments
5. Poor appearance, preventing referral, with lack of improvement within a reasonable period
6. Rejection of reasonable job offers
7. Poor attendance in program
8. Chronic punctuality problems in program
9. Other conditions not listed above that seriously impaired the ability of the client to participate successfully in the program or obtain employment

This could be a double-edged sword, however. Too many rejected clients reduced the intake level, and attainment of the quota was threatened. What seemed to happen was that the definitions were relaxed if intake was lagging, and, if necessary, the staff would actively recruit clients who had been rejected earlier for not keeping appointments, and so on. In 1976 intake into the addict program was lagging primarily because the age of most ex-addicts taken in by the city's various facilities was well above the traditional age limit (21) of the agency—and was even above the special limit allowed for that particular contract, 23 years of age. Addict clients accepted in 1975 were, on average, 28 years old. Counselors assigned to the program were directed to get in touch with younger clients who had been rejected before and to get them back in if possible. Thus, the favorable definitions negotiated for the addict program were of less value when intake lagged, and the agency was forced to re-recruit and accept clients who did not meet one or more of the criteria for acceptance into the program.

SUMMARY

The evidence strongly suggests that YEA directly or indirectly falsified its success rate, both as it is defined here (the placement *rate* for individual clients) and as it was specified in contracts (placement of a given *number* of individuals). The falsification took the form of presenting the total placements, including multiple placements, as though they represented the number of individuals placed.

Alternatively, the agency developed other techniques for promoting or claiming success. These included exploitation of loopholes (especially "double-counting," where the same placement was credited to more than one program), claiming success on peripheral tasks (those not required by the contract), and negotiation of favorable definitions prior to signing the contract. However, these techniques were not needed (though they may have been used) as long as the agency could make acceptable claims for success based on total placements. Despite what appeared to be a vigorous process of verifying placements in the addict program, it was observed that multiple placements were not detected, and YEA was able to advance a credible and acceptable claim for success by making its report imply that the total placements achieved were "clients placed." The integrity of organizational statistics may be questionable under the best of circumstances, but it becomes more so as the organization is pressured for results, particularly when the results are not easily achieved.

NOTES

1. Esther Stanton, *Clients Come Last* (Beverly Hills: Sage, 1970), p. 136–37.

2. This is not meant to deny completely the legitimacy of the reasons advanced. It is reasonable to suppose that the reasons (for example, declining job market) often do have a real bearing on the outcome. We only note that the reasons are given if no basis for success can be found in the way described.

3. The number of placements was considered by the associate director to be lower than usual, due to the decrease in the supply of temporary jobs.

4. The rate of 17.6 percent is based on the formula suggested earlier: the number of clients placed on full-time permanent jobs divided by the number of clients seen.

5. This may be another reason that the administrators did not wish to record and tabulate the placement successes of the counselors. However, if they did do so, they might very well have tabulated the total placements of each counselor by the week or the month or some other period—which is apparently what was done when the placement "quota system" was in effect.

6. Wage rates for clients at that time ran from 55¢ to 70¢ per hour. Salaries paid to clients ranged from $22 to $36 a week.

7. The placement rate of 48 percent, by the more rigorous standard used in this study, would probably be quite acceptable in more recent times.

8. We recall the assertions of Counselor J, who had to "play the same game with OJT" as he did with employers: "Get a few good ones in first, so they will trust my judgment."

6

Contracts and the Mission of YEA

In 1978 an article about YEA appeared in a national magazine.[1] Ten years ago, the article reported, YEA "was able to place 3,000 troubled young people in beginners' jobs. Last year it placed 1,200." The main problem, in the words of YEA's executive director, was that the city was constantly losing jobs, having lost 700,000 in the previous seven years. The agency was said to have contracts with 1,500 companies but found that it had to make 60 phone calls to develop one job, and had to develop four jobs to make one placement.

YEA used to deal with 16 to 21 year olds. It now deals only with teenagers 16 to 19. Of the 2,000 it tried to help last year, 77% were school dropouts, 48% had a known drug or correctional history, 37% had no previous work experience and 18% were receiving public assistance.

Part of the problem was "a breakdown in the criminal justice system and . . . in the educational system as well," YEA's director said. The article continued:

YEA staffers frankly are discouraged. Not only was last year bad but they don't see much sign of improvement. Still they keep trying. The agency, a voluntary organization supported by contributions from individuals, corporations and foundations and government grants, has been in business since 1936. Its mission has always been to help young people, especially those in trouble with the law.

However, the agency was described as now doing more than developing jobs and placing teenagers.

In an effort to stir up some high-level action, it spent $38,000 of its hard-won money last year on a powerful booklet called *Our Turn to Listen* and sent it to senators, congressmen, governors, mayors, and news media all over the country. It pleads for society to get serious about its teenagers' problems, and proposes specific steps to that end.

In the article, the old mission (placement) and what appears to be a new mission involving research, publications, and advocacy are both mentioned. How did this change come about, and how can we relate the change to our main themes?

As a beginning we might say, without attempting to document it here, that the "mission" of a charitable organization such as YEA is extremely important—in establishing priorities, in giving off a sense of purpose to the work and thus motivating the personnel, and even in selling the services of the agency. When the mission is forgotten, the organization might as well close its doors. There is no longer any life in it.

There is a tendency, however, to confuse what the organization *does* with its "mission." This was true at YEA, as we shall see, and, in fact, the research and analysis reported here was guided by this misconception for some time. The mission seemed to be placement, finding jobs for young people who had "been in trouble with the law," and so forth. This proved not to be the case. Eventually it became clear that the mission lay in providing some *unique* service for a given client population (young, in trouble with the law, and so forth), not in the specific service of job placement. If we can view it this way, the developments at YEA make sense; that is, we are not required to invent reasons why persons would abandon activities that were of great importance to them. The "custodian" of the mission at YEA was, of course, the chairman, and he is focused on in this chapter.

In *Clients Come Last*, Stanton describes a mental health agency where the overall and policy-making power of the board of directors was an illusion. The professional staff, while formally de-emphasized and subordinate, constituted the "informal organization" that in fact determined as well as implemented policy. Board members had "neither the time nor the inclination to handle the complexities of programs entailing months of preparation and the coordination of hundreds of volunteers."[2] She also observed that "since the Board of Directors is reorganized annually, it is management which comes and goes and the employees who must train (and sometimes even select) the administration."[3]

At YEA, by contrast, the chairman was the permanent member of the organization. Executive directors and staff came and went. The chairman of the board had the legal authority of his position but also, as the "patron" of many board members, he had economic and personal power over the majority of members. As a principal economic benefactor of the agency he had power added to his authority over staff.

And as founder of the agency he had both the interest and the inclination to exercise his authority and power.

In recent years the chairman and other board members had expressed concern that the agency was too dependent upon outside government agencies and contractors. The danger was that the agency would
become so involved in the pursuit of new contracts and a mania for
growth that it would lose any sense of its own purpose. The proliferation of contracts and their growing command over the agency's operations was seen to threaten the agency's mission.

In August 1974 the agency convened a meeting in its new conference
room. Two days were devoted to what was called the "Assessment and
Goals Conference on Youth and Work." Those participating in the conference included Center City's commissioner for the Department of
Employment (which channeled virtually all local, state, and federal
manpower funds) and the assistant regional director of the U.S. Department of Labor (who headed the labor-statistics section). Also attending were an academic affiliated with a prominent university in the
city, the executive vice president of Center City's Economic Development Council (a private, business-oriented group), the executive director of the local manpower planning council (composed of public and
voluntary agencies), and a bank official. The purpose of the conference
was to deal with three questions:

1. What is the true magnitude of the unemployment problem among youth?
2. What has been the current response of the public and private sectors to the
   problem?
3. What has been the effectiveness and impact of YEA's contribution, and in
   light of the two previous questions, what direction should the agency's future role assume?

We need not be concerned with all details of the conference. However, we may observe that all the participants had suggestions as to
what YEA should do. For example, the Economic Development Council official emphasized the economic nature of the problems YEA faced.
That is, until the economic situation in Center City turned around, the
agency was "pushing on a marshmallow" and was in the "wrong business." The agency was urged to be "more politically active in order to
make economic development . . . a desirable reality," by testifying before local government bodies and involving itself "in the overall political, business, and economic-development" climate of the city.

The academic researcher discussed the historical rationing of jobs by
age, sex, and so on and the non-competitiveness of youth labor. She
also discussed the need for "shepherding" young workers (face-to-face

contact: "seeing that they have something constructive to do until, with age, they outgrow their youth").

"Shepherding" was a concept that appealed to the city's employment commissioner. She used it as an example of the type of innovative effort her agency was willing to fund, and she virtually invited YEA to submit a proposal. Other panelists presented other interpretations of the problem and what YEA should do. The "solutions" ranged all the way from recognizing impotence to radical redefinition of mission and activities.

On the second day of the conference, YEA administrators and board members struggled with the problem of what to make of all this advice and information. The executive director urged that the agency seek a new uniqueness through innovative programs which it would "advocate" as models for others (though he was not yet ready to abandon the more fundable "original mission"). In the director's view, "the agency will no longer remain successful if it continues to operate exclusively as a placement service."

The board members were divided in their opinions. One observed that "as long as YEA is doing what it is doing well, I haven't been 'losing a lot of sleep' about not being unique." The president of YEA observed that the agency was "in a very serious dilemma" due to the number of unemployed youths, the competition from other public and private agencies for jobs for clients, and the political structure of city government which made obtaining funds a struggle. He argued that YEA had to go "one of three routes." It must either seek "large, massive contracts with the Federal, State, and City governments thereby eliminating the private nature of the organization"; work with fewer clients "more on a social work basis, as YEA did 10–12 years ago," taking satisfaction from helping fewer individuals in the best way it could; or else "seek public and private funds to become an 'advocate' on behalf of the youth population." In that case "the agency would serve the same population, and serve to attack the same problem, but in a different role." The former executive director of YEA emphasized that "no matter how sophisticated the agency gets, no matter what its political 'clout,' no matter how much money it gets, if it doesn't meet the youngster's real needs, it doesn't have to be in business."

The chairman spoke last. He pointed out that the agency had a "unique opportunity to be a leader for dialogue in the field of youth employment if it is decided that YEA's contribution should be more substantial than just job placement." The idea of advocacy should be considered, he said, because it "attracts attention to itself," and because it "focuses other people on this field in an effective way." He expressed appreciation for the employment commissioner's suggestion about engaging in innovative followup programs. He added, however, that he did not want "to see the organization become a conglomerate unless for a specific purpose which fits within the focus and pattern of the overall mission" of the agency.

In February 1975 a report titled *Civil Disabilities of Ex-Offenders* was put out by a research group set up by the agency for the purpose of conducting and publishing the study. The executive director of YEA was one of the three investigators listed. Funds for the study were provided by a foundation whose president is also YEA's president. The study appears to have had two purposes: (1) To cover part of the executive director's salary at YEA at a time when the agency's budget was difficult to balance, and (2) to explore the waters of "advocacy." This concept had been discussed previously by YEA's president and its chairman. At that time, "advocacy" of the problems and needs of "youth in trouble" may have been seen as supplementary to direct service for such clients. The research group did a mail survey of the employers in YEA's files and interviewed approximately 500 "ex-offenders." The results were not widely disseminated, but it was a first step in moving the agency toward "advocacy."

In a 1975 meeting at YEA, the chairman learned that the average age of the clients in the addict program was 28; he also was told the criteria for "correctional" cases were sometimes "stretched" by the agency to enable some clients to qualify for certain services in the crime-prevention program. The staff member who disclosed this information may have assumed that the chairman already knew about it. In any event, the board issued a public statement shortly thereafter announcing that YEA's "original mission" was more important than ever. More specifically, the agency was instructed to limit its services to clients who were 16 to 19 years old and who were school dropouts and had "some correctional history." The statement began by noting that for 40 years the agency had "taken as its single challenge one of the most intractable problems of modern society," the young unemployed dropout who was "in trouble with the law." The agency's goal had "been simple: to find jobs for these men and women." Despite the agency's past successes, new problems had emerged: Economic and social conditions in the city had "deteriorated significantly," and consequently "the city's pool of unskilled, inexperienced young people continued to grow," contributing to "soaring crime rates, the spread of drug addiction, burgeoning welfare rolls, and a growing sense of alienation and despair."

The statement noted that during the past few years the agency had "done more work on a contract basis for government agencies" and that as part of this expansion, YEA had been asked "to broaden its activities beyond direct job placement into training and general counseling, and beyond troubled teenagers to include adults and those who do not come from correctional backgrounds." However, recent cutbacks in "public monies" for employment programs had forced YEA "to ask some hard questions about its priorities."

The directors concluded: "Our answer now is clear. We believe YEA should focus even more sharply on its original and basic mission" even though this might mean "foregoing certain grants which carry other perhaps more achievable priorities." The mission was defined as "finding jobs for 16 to 19 year old boys and girls who are out of school, and with some correctional history." The statement ended on a note of determination:

YEA will hold to this course for as long as we are able. We believe that a society that provides work and education for all its people is a proud, healthy and honorable society, and to that end we pledge our resources and our faith.

Funding cutbacks as well as the drift of the organization had prompted the board to consider anew the question of mission. For the time being, the board's answer was to strongly reaffirm the agency's original mission, even narrowing it by restricting services to clients who were under 19.

"THE PROJECT": CONSIDERATION OF A NEW MISSION

Shortly after reaffirming the mission of the agency, the board began to experiment in earnest with defining what appeared to be a new mission. There had been earlier discussions of the agency's purpose in the new environment of federal programs. But this question took on a new urgency. The "Project," as it was called, was the chairman's creation. In a memo dated December 2, 1976, to the executive director and the president of YEA, the chairman outlined the "unique [and] dramatic mission" of the undertaking. "The premise on which we started the YEA project," he noted, was the "sharp increase in crime in the major cities . . . an increase in the seriousness of the crimes committed . . . and the increase in the participation in these crimes by youngsters in the 16–19 year age bracket." The agency had been dealing with this constituency for 40 years, the chairman noted. Thus, it was ideally suited to undertake the project he had in mind. The purpose of the project was "to elicit from a representative group of our clients *their* views as to what causes this increase in crime in major cities—why the increase in the seriousness of crime, particularly against persons—and what brings about the increase in participation by the 16–19 year age group." There already existed numerous opinions as to the causes of the problem, he acknowledged, but "no one heard from this age group as to their opinion." The Project would be "a unique mission—a dramatic mission," the chairman asserted.

The plan for the project was to videotape a group of clients discussing the problem of youth crime. The videotapes were to be analyzed and used as the basis for a "white paper" on the problem. The possibility of editing and preparing the tapes for showing on television was also mentioned, although that was "icing on the cake." The "cake" was to be the report, which would be distributed to legislators, administrators, and other advocacy groups.

Filming for the Project began in the fall of 1976 and was still going on the following summer. An article about this work appeared in one of the city's newspapers.

David is a 19-year-old high school dropout with a police record who spends most of his time on the streets looking for a job or a victim.

He says he would like to tell the State Legislature about the frustration faced by youths like him who are poorly educated, out of work, out of money and who turn to street crimes because they say it is the only way to survive.

To meet this need, the Youth Employment Agency is providing a forum through which they can address decision-making administrators, businessmen and advocacy groups in a position to respond to their call for help.[4]

The article then went on to describe the videotaping and the uses planned for the material. "It is perhaps the first time that youths are telling us what their problems are," the director said. Heretofore, he said, "we have been saturated by the sociologists' view of what the youths want and what their needs are."

The "white paper" resulting from the effort was published in 1977 and was entitled *Our Turn to Listen*. Based upon "115 hours of interviews with more than 100 of YEA's clients and a wide range of outside experts," the study was edited into a half-hour film and the white paper.

Listen to their voices. Speaking of survival and violence, sickness and even starvation, hopelessness and homelessness, expressing a profound and implacable cynicism. Child prodigies of despair. Listen to them. They are Americans and they will not go away. They are gathering and festering joblessly in all our major cities. As time passes, they become ever more deeply estranged from the laws and the institutions of our society.

Some of them line up daily at Youth Employment Agency. For 40 years YEA has specialized in finding jobs for troubled young people—nearly 3,000 of them every year. Never in YEA's long history have the jobs been so few, the young people so troubled, and YEA's leadership so frightened by the condition of their queued-up clientele. The staff, collectively representing more than a century of experience in dealing with youth unemployment, is ready for the first time to declare a state of emergency—to declare that the problem is beyond their reach.

In the interviews, the young voices rise in angry rejection of all the usual pieties, be they liberal or conservative, that get invoked to explain their plight— from laziness and welfare glut to a need for more schooling. They denounce most of the favored programs, the doles and therapies, that are designed to improve their lives but more often stultify rather than help them.

The paper cited the testimony of clients, concluding with a list of 10 "key barriers" to the job market for "ghetto young people" and pro- posing 10 "barrier breakers" for alleviating the problem. The barrier breakers focused upon the need for governmental action to alleviate or change the laws and the business, governmental, and union practices cited. In education, for example, it proposed to "make departure from school at age 16 coincide with the completion of a certifiable phase of education" so that widespread use of the high school diploma as a "passport to the job market" would no longer be such a formidable barrier. Enlarged use of community development corporations was ad- vocated so as to "promote the development of small businesses," which tend to hire more unskilled workers. Also, the "privatization of certain governmental functions" was advocated, so as to facilitate the employ- ment of youths for such jobs as rebuilding city neighborhoods, improv- ing public parks and facilities, and providing services to older and de- pendent people.

The Project represented not a new "mission" for the agency but new tasks utilizing new techniques and skills, aimed at serving the same client groups as always. In this, there was no need for counselors. Place- ment, as part of the agency's work, could be abandoned. The type of funding YEA had demonstrated it could obtain would be given up, adding an even greater element of insecurity. And there had been re- luctance to break with certain important traditions and purposes. But the problems of Center City (especially the decline of manufacturing jobs and the acute competition for placement into low-skilled jobs gen- erally) and the seemingly permanent intervention of government in manpower programs forced a reconsideration of what the agency should do and why.

Up to the present the mission of YEA has involved direct services, such as job placement, rendered to "youth in trouble." The Project did not change the mission, however. The process of redirecting the mis- sion, as we saw, involved only one of the variables mentioned—"ser- vices rendered." The target population would remain the same. YEA's chairman and its director apparently have concluded that the agency, while successful in the past fulfilling the mission in one way (direct services such as job placement to individual clients), may not be successful in the future if the same means are used.

The counselors were not enthusiastic about either of the events described in this chapter. Limiting services to younger clients was seen as foolhardy, making their placement more difficult because older clients would not be available to "open the door" of employers. Similarly, restricting the clientele to correctional cases was in opposition to the counselors' concern for other types of disadvantaged clients. The counselors did not openly criticize the Project, even though its success would portend the elimination of their jobs. Instead, they disparaged and joked about the "media types" in dark glasses who suddenly descended upon the agency.

A change in the services provided by YEA could conceivably be very desirable and beneficial for all concerned. We cannot judge that here. We can only describe how the agency was led to consider new services of an advocacy nature, as well as the possibility of no longer providing job placement for its clientele—and how these developments were related to our interest in the ramifications of YEA's contractual relations. The connection seemed to be a very direct one, growing out of the board's concern (particularly of the chairman) that it was losing control over the agency and losing sight of its mission.

NOTES

1. See *Forbes*, May 15, 1978.

2. Esther Stanton, *Clients Come Last: Volunteers and Welfare Organizations* (Beverly Hills: Sage Publications, 1970), p. 67.

3. Ibid., p. 72.

4. *New York Times*, November 8, 1976.

7

Weeding Out the Target Population

The Faustian bargain made by YEA—for the purpose of expanding its program and enhancing the reputation of the agency—was not fully satisfied by the loss of integrity in its reports and the diminution of control over its mission. In December 1972 a letter from YEA's executive director was published in one of the city's newspapers:[1] "The Dec. 11 editorial noting the drop in the unemployment rate quite correctly pointed out the discrepancy between the white worker and the black worker, the older worker and the teenager. To be black and young is economically disastrous." What is to be done? he asked. The letter contained a number of suggestions. Part of the problem, however, was the Department of Labor.

Too often the Government's criteria in manpower funding are based on immediate placement, filling slots and job retention, rather than on the long-range needs of the individual or the community. Inflexibility in manpower funding precludes effective program operation and experimentation.

In 1973 the agency began its first large contract program involving detailed performance standards, with job placement and retention quotas, a monthly timetable, and penalties for substandard performance. Table 7.1 compares the three-year period prior to 1973 and the three-year period after 1973, with respect to the percentages of clients who did not return after one interview. The figures are derived from a sample of the agency's files.

The substantial increase in the percentage of "one-interview clients" suggests that clients were being increasingly "weeded out"—that is, not retrieved for service. Interviews with the counselors showed that this was accomplished by leaving it up to the client to "keep in touch" with the counselor, the purpose of which was to test the client's "motivation." In the earlier period (prior to 1973) counselors assumed respon-

Table 7.1
Percentage of Clients Not Returning after One Interview

Period	One Interview Only
1970-1972	17% (6/36)
1974-1976	41% (22/54)

sibility for maintaining contact with clients and encouraging them with job openings. At that time, counselors were expected to maintain a list of clients who were "available for work," along with the type of job desired and the clients' traits and skills. When a suitable job was available, the counselor put a "hold" on the job and contacted the client by phone. Clients who did not return after the first interview were thus not necessarily deprived of a job. Counselors seemed to work harder at keeping in touch with the client and in encouraging them with job offers. The "available-for-work system" was based, in part, on the belief that clients were not sufficiently motivated to come to the agency's office frequently in the quest for a job. Contracts merely stipulated that the agency would accept a given number of clients referred to it by the funding agency (a government department) and would make its "best effort" to place them on jobs. Contracts of the best-effort type were typical of the 1970–72 period and are associated with the low rate of "one-interview clients" in the table.

By 1976, however, clients were required to keep in touch with the agency's counselors in order to be considered for job placement. Jobs were not held for clients, and clients were persuaded to take any job that was available regardless of their interests, backgrounds, or experience. Extensive observations of the counselors at work in 1976 showed, for example, that one counselor received five incoming phone calls in one morning while making two outgoing calls. The incoming calls were from clients who were checking on the availability of jobs—that is, keeping in touch. Judging from the conversations, even the outgoing calls (reporting on possible jobs) were to clients who had been keeping in touch with the counselor. Another counselor was observed to mention the importance of keeping in touch four times during the course of a single client interview. Still another counselor advised a client that "showing us you want to do something for yourself means keeping in touch."

The process of weeding out certain clients who were hard to place because they were "not motivated" was an ongoing cumulative process. It began with the counselor's attempt to form "character judgments" about the client, usually in the first session. The next stage, "keeping in touch," was regarded as being a critical test of the client's motivations. Keeping in touch was measured by whether the client called in to inquire about the availability of jobs. A related but independent indicator was whether the client kept appointments with the counselor. Later, the client's performance in showing up for job interviews was used: "NSU" in the client's folder, next to a referral entry, meant that the client "never showed up." Finally, there was performance on the job itself when the client was placed. This was often used to gauge "motivation" or "work readiness." If the client was fired because of absenteeism, he was not ready for work. Similarly, if the client quit the job because of boredom he was adjudged to be lacking in either motivation or work readiness.

Clients could atone for failure to keep appointments with the counselor if they called in advance or called in with a credible excuse—provided they did not do this often. Similarly, failure to show up for job interviews could be excused if the client subsequently kept in touch. Failure to perform adequately on the job appeared to be the easiest one to compensate for by continuing to keep in touch. Keeping in touch thus appeared to be the most crucial behavior for clients if they wished to be placed on a job. An explanation of this was provided by Counselor J. He was asked: How do you deal with the frustration of not being able to do something for everybody who comes into your office? "That's when the love (of the work) comes in," he replied. He then continued: "Also, understanding that there are logistic problems involved, in terms of time and caseload, is necessary. You *try*. Obviously, you go with the intention of helping every single client. But then you have to slowly eliminate some—through just weeding out those who really do not want a job."

Are they the ones who don't come back or don't call you? he was asked. He responded: "Right . . . . When they come to us, they should be ready for work, and you go on that assumption until he shows you something else . . . . It's difficult to read their minds." Some clients, he said, showed by their behavior in the interview that they may not have been ready for work: "If the kid is just sitting there, looking up at the ceiling and hitting on the table, indirectly, the kid is telling you to go fuck yourself."

Sometimes, he said, he found it necessary to "cut the interview, give him my card and say, 'When you feel you are ready, give me a call.' " At YEA, he said, it was very difficult to deal with such clients because "there's a lot of hidden things behind that negativeness" that would require "a lot of time that you don't have here" to understand. He concluded: "This is what I'm saying in terms of you have to weed out. You're forced to weed out. And the thing that's really ironic about it is that that's the one that needs help the most."

Counselor G, when asked about the clients' obligations in the relationship with the counselor, replied that keeping appointments was one of them, "if they're really serious about working."

Counselor F was asked if keeping in touch was one of the clients' obligations. "That is probably the major one," she said. She also mentioned "coming in on time and letting me know if they are going to be late."

Examination of all the sample cases seen in 1974–76 suggested that at least three variables could be used to characterize the clients who were weeded out in all programs. These are *age*, *education*, and *work experience*. The findings are summarized in Table 7.2. Sixty-four percent of all clients in the sample of cases studied who were 18 years old or younger had one interview only, compared with 25 percent for the older clients.

Analysis of the sample also showed that the clients who were weeded out had less education than the others, as shown in Table 7.3. In addition, only 10 percent (2 out of 20) of the "one-interview clients" had 12 years of education, while 23 percent of the others had at least a high school education. A few of the latter had some college. These clients also had somewhat less work experience. The comparison is shown in Table 7.4.

The number of jobs refers to those jobs held prior to going to the agency. The difference here is not striking, though it must be noted that most clients had relatively little work experience recorded. Within that context, small differences may be more important. It may also be true that other factors such as kind of job held and duration of previous employment were important influences on the counselors' retrieval efforts aimed at individual clients. However, no analysis of these factors has been made.

In general, it appeared that the counselors' test for motivation (keeping in touch) increasingly weeded out the clients who needed help the most: the youngest, the least educated, and the least experienced. The change occurred at about the same time that the agency was making the transition to a new type of contract. The new contracts did not completely eliminate the counselors' client-retrieval efforts, but apparently the effort was more selective and was focused upon clients sufficiently motivated to keep in touch with the counselor. Frequently, it was the younger, less educated and less experienced client who did not pass this test of motivation.

An effort has been made to see what the relationship might be between keeping in touch and placement, using as a sample those clients who were interviewed for the study. Of the 13 clients in this sample,[2] five were judged to have made no effort to keep in touch, four made what was regarded as a minimal effort, and four made a sustained effort. The effort was judged according to entries in the folders.[3] If the

Table 7.2
Client Age and "Weeding Out"

AGE	NUMBER OF INTERVIEWS		
	One	One Plus	Total
18 or under	14 (64%)	8 (36%)	22 (100%)
19 or over	8 (25%)	24 (75%)	32 (100%)

Table 7.3
Client Education and "Weeding Out"

NUMBER OF INTERVIEWS	MEAN YEARS OF EDUCATION
One	9.7
More than one	10.7

Table 7.4
Client Work Experience and "Weeding Out"

NUMBER OF INTERVIEWS	MEAN NO. OF JOBS
One	1.3
More than one	1.85

client did not return (after registration) for the first counseling session, or returned only for the first session but no further contact was recorded, he or she was considered to have made no effort. If the client returned once or twice after the first session, or called in, this was considered minimal effort. Anything beyond that is considered to be sustained effort. The findings are summarized in Table 7.5.

Except for two clients in the minimal-effort category who were placed immediately, it seemed that placement was directly dependent upon "keeping in touch," as might be expected. The counselors did not "track down" clients who failed to keep in touch. Without keeping in touch, there was no chance of the client's getting a job, unless he or she was fortunate enough to get one at the first interview.

STRATEGY IN THE FIRST COUNSELING SESSION

Although the counselors claimed to rely principally upon the clients' behavior to judge "character" and to "weed out" those who were not

Table 7.5
Relationship between Keeping in Touch and Placement

	Client Effort to Keep in Touch		
Placement	None (N=5)	Minimal (N=4)	Sustained (N=4)
Yes		2	3
No	5	2	1*

*This client was only interested in hospital work. The counselor asserted that the agency did not have access to such jobs.

motivated and job-ready, they did not wait for this information before beginning to work on the client. The first task appeared to be to educate the client about the realities of the job market and his or her chances of getting a job and, at the same time, building up the client's hopes for obtaining a job of some kind even if it was not the most desirable job.

The evidence is not as clear as we might desire on the relationship between the client's estimate of his or her chances of getting a job and the effort made to keep in touch with the counselor; it does suggest, however, that clients left the first counseling session with a lower estimate of their chances of getting a job they would have "liked"—and with a higher estimate of their chances of "getting a job of some kind."

The clients in the sample to be interviewed were asked—before any services were provided by the agency—to estimate their chances of "getting a job you would like" and their chances of "getting any kind of job." There were four choices: very good, good, fair, and poor. Those clients who returned the following day for counseling were asked the same questions after they had talked with the counselor.

When clients were asked to estimate their chances of getting a job they "would like," their responses showed a pattern of decreasing optimism after the first counseling session. Of the nine clients whose interviews were usable on this item, two rated their chances as improved after the initial counseling session, two indicated no change, and five believed they had less chance of a desirable job.

There was no consistent connection between the perceived chances of getting a desirable job and the *effort* clients made to keep in touch. Of the two whose perceived chances increased, one made no effort and one made a sustained effort to keep in touch. Of the five whose perceived chances decreased, one made no effort to keep in touch, while the others made either minimal or sustained efforts. If the initial counseling session resulted in a lowered optimism about getting a *desirable* job, it seemed to increase the clients' estimates of getting a job of some kind.

Here, the evidence showed that five out of seven of the clients on whom the information was available felt that their chances of getting a job of some kind improved after the first counseling session. These tended to be the same clients who saw less chance of getting a desirable job, suggesting that the usual pattern is for clients to be educated about the realities of the job market and their place in it. Thus, they were cooled off, becoming less optimistic about getting a job they would like and were simultaneously "motivated" by the counselor to seek a job of some kind. If this is so, we might suppose that such encouragement induces "effort." Of the five clients whose perceived chances of getting a job of some kind went *up* after counseling, all made at least a minimal effort to keep in touch and two of them made a sustained effort. The one client who reported seeing *less chance* of getting this kind of job also made a sustained effort, but inasmuch as the client was interested only in hospital work, which the counselor told her was quite unlikely, her perceived chances may have responded to this factor alone.

Although based on a very small number of cases, the implication of this finding is that despite their avowed practice of weeding out clients based upon the clients' behavior, the counselors influenced, more than they acknowledged, the effort the clients made to keep in touch by the degree of encouragement they offered to clients as early as in the first session. If "effort" is correlated with placement (as we observed earlier), and if "encouragement" is correlated with effort (as suggested here), then the placement process and the attainment of success were not as much due to the clients' motivation and effort as the counselors believed.

If the counselors' intended strategy in the early stage was to weed out clients based on their behavior, their *actual* and unintentional strategy was to simultaneously deflate the clients' long-term aspirations and inflate their immediate hopes of working, that is, making the client both more realistic and more optimistic and willing to accept the jobs that were available. And the more "realistic" the client was, the better the chances of being placed. This was in direct opposition to the agency's mission, of course, and was contrary to the purposes of the contract programs as well.

YEA's mission, strongly influenced by the views of its founder and long-time board chairman, was to help young juvenile offenders and dropouts avoid criminal careers by offering them job counseling and placement. The mission had survived the transition from a predominantly white clientele in the 1930s and the post-war period to one that in recent years was composed largely of minority groups. In the 1950s YEA was an important organization in the city's campaign to "socialize" the youthful gangs that were prevalent at the time. The agency had adjusted its intake standards in the 1960s to accommodate the "disadvantaged" client as well as the youthful offender, but its primary purpose was still thought to be serving the latter group. They were young and hard to place, and YEA viewed itself as being unique in its concern for them.

The practice of weeding out certain clients was similar in some ways to the goal displacement observed by Blau at a state employment service.[4] Blau centers his attention on the internal workings of the agency he studied. In Chapter 3 he describes the organizational dysfunctions that resulted from the introduction of statistical performance records by a new supervisor in the employment agency. Eight indexes of performance were measured (and reported to the counselors themselves). These were considered in the evaluation of the counselors. The indexes were:

1. The number of interviews held
2. The number of clients referred to a job
3. The number of placements made
4. The proportion of interviews resulting in referrals
5. The proportion of referrals resulting in placements
6. The proportion of interviews resulting in placements
7. The number of notifications sent to the unemployment insurance office
8. The number of application forms made out

"The introduction of these records," concluded Blau, "improved placement operations considerably."[5] The statistical reports induced the counselors "to concentrate their efforts on the factors that were measured and thus would affect their rating."[6] While counselors "often protested that the 'statistics' measured only 'quantity' and not 'quality,' " Blau concluded that the "accusation was not justified," since the performance records measured whether "certain objectives [such as placements] were accomplished."[7]

The functional consequences of the performance records were that they increased productivity, facilitated hierarchical control, enabled superiors to institute changes in operations quickly and effectively, and improved the relations between supervisors and counselors, since the records reduced the need for supervisors to "criticize subordinates."[8]

The dysfunctional consequences of the performance records were that they reduced the supervisory function to a clerical level and thus posed a threat to their authority; and they led to "displacement of goals," as counselors tried to "maximize their figures" by various means, thus subverting certain goals of the agency.[9] In addition, they adversely affected the "interpersonal relations among interviewers" (counselors) including an increase in competition.[10]

In short, the employment counselors observed by Blau did what they were told to do if it was measured, included in their performance evaluations, and (presumably) rewarded. On the surface, YEA's counselors appeared to be doing the same thing. One important difference, however, was that work measurements and performance records of the type described by Blau did not exist at YEA. Placement quotas were tried briefly in 1974 and abandoned. The principal counselors' strategy at YEA was one that was initiated by the counselors themselves, rather than being influenced by the directives of superiors, as described by Blau.[11] Instead, the counselors seem to have internalized the standards imposed on the agency. The practice of weeding out clients at YEA was to largely eliminate from service the very clients whom the agency intended to help—a more far-reaching effect than the service reductions Blau noted.

EVALUATION OF YEA'S COUNSELORS

The agency's unwillingness to evaluate the counselors' work consistently and systematically, counselors' opinions to the contrary, was a puzzle. The agency as a whole was evaluated by such standards. Why should it not evaluate and reward its counselors in the same way?

The agency did implement a placement evaluation system in 1975, but it was imposed for only two or three months. Each counselor was supposed to make five placements per week. As we saw earlier, the system was abandoned because it was said to be causing too much conflict among the counselors. Neither of the two top administrators seemed to know if placements went up or down as a result of the "quota system." They talked about it as something they would rather forget about.

The associate director said that evaluation of counselors "depends on many factors" such as the job market, though there was a level of placements below which no one should go. He also argued that one "cannot look at limited time spans—a day, a week" in evaluating a counselor's work. There were too many uncontrollable fluctuations. The quota system was not "punitive" in intent, he said, but because of the "fear element" deriving from the director's "methodology"—his ways of dealing with people—the counselors interpreted the system as punitive.

The quota system was thus considered to be a failure. The counselors did not like it. The associate director had probably never liked the idea. And the director was not sold on it sufficiently to hold out against all the resistance. In addition, one of the victims of the system was one of the female counselors whom he liked. She had the highest placement rate under the system but was "ostracized" by other counselors as a result.

The counselors had no clear alternatives for dealing with the evaluation problem. They were not happy with the uncertainty of the present system but were troubled by precise measurements of their work. In 1976, a meeting between the Staff Council and the director was held. The Staff Council was elected by the counseling staff to deal with the administration on grievances, work conditions, and so on. The Staff Council developed in the aftermath of the abortive unionization.[12] The record of the meeting indicates that the counselors did not endorse a quota system, yet they could advance no criterion other than effort, the same method used by agency administrators to evaluate counselors, now and in the past. One counselor said at the meeting: "Who is performing and who is not should be obvious to supervisors without counting placements. If a colleague who is obviously trying to make placements and is falling short . . . their fellow workers should try to find out the problem and help that counselor." Much of this meeting was devoted to discussing the criteria by which counselors and job developers were evaluated. "What is the rating system?" was the question asked at the meeting. The counselors were reportedly in agreement in asking: "If people are on staff on a permanent basis [that is, not on probation], doesn't everyone have a satisfactory rating?"

At the time research for this study was terminated, the agency had two means for evaluating the work of counselors. These were the "annual evaluations" and a "review of placement statistics." The associate director described the latter as a "countdown somewhere of each counselor's activity—of raw placements." But, he added, "I don't keep up with it each month." There is no evidence indicating that these figures were used at all. If they were used in the "annual" evaluations, there appears to be no standard against which they were measured.

The annual evaluations covered three areas: punctuality, job performance, and "attitude and growth outlook." The most recent evaluations of Counselor J and Counselor G are summarized below. Both of these counselors were retained after the May 1976 layoffs. However, Counselor J was scheduled to be laid off at the end of June 1976 if no new funds were obtained, despite what appeared to be a good rating on most items. It is not possible to say with any certainty whether this had any relationship to his union and staff council roles. We can observe that there are numerous "good effort" qualifiers in the evaluations. These appear to be indicators that performance in these areas was not all that it should have been.

Punctuality was evaluated in terms of reporting to work on time and adhering to the "lunch hour policy" (that is, taking no more than an hour for lunch). Counselor J, it was noted, had "difficulty in arriving to work on time" but showed attempts "to make up for the loss in time by working late." Counselor G was said to make a "good effort in reporting on time." Neither counselor was guilty of frequently taking long lunches.

Job performance was evaluated in terms of keeping client records up to date, the counselor's placement rate, turning in reports on time, establishing rapport with clients, relations with employers, and promptness in seeing clients when they arrived. Counselor J's evaluation stated that his record-keeping was "usually up to date," although it was noted that his "style in writing could be better." This counselor's placement rate was described as being "excellent." Counselor G, on the other hand, was cautioned that his record entries were "very brief," and that there was "limited explanation of client activity shown." His placement rate was characterized as "acceptable." Both counselors were said to make "good effort" toward handing in reports on time, to have good rapport with clients and employers, and to see clients soon after arrival.

"Attitude and growth outlook" was evaluated according to the counselor's relationship with other staff members, attitude in the performance of duties, "acceptance of direction" from supervisors, independent decision-making ability, and interest shown in the work. Both of these counselors met these standards, according to their evaluations.

We should note two features of the evaluations. Most of the items are either not measurable or are not measured. Exceptions to this are attendance and punctuality. Other items are based on the supervisor's impressions and on the absence of negative information—for example, with respect to rapport. Thus, even with the institutionalization of formal evaluations, the agency resisted the measurement of work.[13] The evaluation can be seen as really assessing (or attempting to do so) only a few things. These are technique, decision-making ability, attitude toward work and agency, and "busy-ness."

Decision-making ability is of minor importance, being represented by one item. Technique is assessed by "placement rate" and "rapport"— neither of which is observable or measured.[14] The majority of items— and the most observable ones—thus assess two things: *attitude* and what is referred to here as "busy-ness." It is not always easy to distinguish between the two: "Handing reports in on time" might be said to represent a desired attitude about timely reports as much as it reflects the busy-ness necessary to do the reports on time. In other cases, the differences are a little clearer: "Accepts direction" is an evaluation of attitude; "reporting to work on time" is an evaluation of (full-time) busy-ness. The items are classified in the table according to whether they appear to represent evaluations of "attitude" or "busy-ness."

Attitude	*Busy-ness*

Attitude

1. "interest in his work"
2. "accepts direction"
3. "willingly performs assignments
4. "good relationship with co-workers"

Busy-ness

1. "reporting to work on time"
2. adhering to lunch-hour policy
3. maintaining records
4. good effort in accomplishing placement goal
5. timely reports
6. "sees clients soon"

Just as counselors "weeded out" clients who were not "motivated" and did not "keep in touch," administrators and supervisors appeared to classify and rate counselors according to whether they kept busy. Lacking any other acceptable standards of performance, busy-ness became the operating standard. It both expressed the attitude desired by the agency and embodied the associate director's belief that the counselors would make placements if they kept busy. "I can't believe," he said, "that if there are jobs out there, the counselors won't send the kids out." And if there were jobs, all that remained was to see that the counselors kept busy. Attendance and punctuality and taking no more than the prescribed lunch hour became more important. More attention was given to this category of standards than to any other.

However, when all counselors were busy, other, more subtle standards of evaluation were required (and employed) to discriminate among counselors. These are not easily classifiable: They appear to reflect evaluations of attitude as directly perceived; they also involve other things such as the appearance of and style of work preferred by supervisors. There was considerable uncertainty for the counselors: Until the standards were discerned, virtually any act might represent "failure" in the eyes of the superiors.

The following material, from the interview with Counselor F, illustrates (1) the importance of busy-ness (here in the form of not talking with other counselors), (2) uncertainty over the more subtle standards of evaluation, and (3) the role of third-party messages in communicating unacceptable performance.

Counselor F was asked about the staff's decision to affiliate with a union. In response, she mentioned the many "personal" and unique reasons various counselors had. "There is a *mood* here—of intrigue—unlike any place I've ever worked," she said. The counselor continued: "I know when I came here, I was told not to be too friendly with people because you can't trust anybody. Now this is one of the administrators saying this to me! . . . At times, it came down to particular people." The counselor recalled an incident that had angered the associate director:

He saw me talking to a fellow counselor that I did spend a lot of time talking with about work—and instead of coming right out and saying "OK, break it up!," he got very upset and went into H____'s office and said, "Break them up! Right now!" He was really angry. So I went to see him and said, "I really want to talk this out. It's very upsetting to me. I've never had a problem at any job in my life . . . . I work hard, etc." He agreed with all that. But he kept saying, "Well, it's appearances [that count]—blah, blah." There's a big thing about appearances here.

  The counselor was then asked if any of the counselors seemed to be successful in predicting what pleased the administrators. She replied that everyone who "survived the layoff must please them in some way. But I don't know in what way." She then returned to the subject of third-party messages: "I have almost never gotten any information directly to my face—about my work, my own 'style,' whatever. It has always been oblique or third hand."

Earlier in the interview the counselor was asked how her work was evaluated. She replied that "placement was part of it" but was not a major part. "Work is really evaluated very subjectively here," she stated. "I'm not even sure that it's work that is being evaluated here." What then? she was asked. "Style," she said, "professionally and personally." Her supervisor, she said, wanted her to seek her advice about client problems, and "she loves to get involved." For this reason, the counselor made a point of "going in with some relatively minor problem, and chatting." She added: "If you just sit in your office and work very, very hard and make lots of placements—that's not the whole thing."

The associate director cited "productivity" and "attitudes" as factors in deciding whom to lay off after the addict program was not funded again. Productivity apparently did not primarily mean placement success. In describing the reasons for laying off one particular counselor, the associate director charged that his reports were not turned in on time, he was a "clown" (that is, he clowned around), he talked too much with other counselors and staff, and he made too many personal phone calls. He summarized, "We all liked him. He would promise to change, but after a while, he would slide back again."

The agency's reluctance to fire counselors added to the uncertainty. The counselors could not easily gauge the limits of tolerated behavior. The associate director, continuing to discuss the counselor who was laid off, pointed out that the agency had delayed firing him, gave him additional chances, spoke to him, warned him—but all failed. He said, "You had to keep after him. He was tottering constantly. The layoff was an ideal opportunity to get rid of him."

The situation, for counselors, involved a great deal of ambivalence and uncertainty. They wanted to know that there were standards and what the standards were, in order to relieve the uncertainty. Yet they also wanted the standards to be vague, based on such intangibles as effort and the quality of one's work. The agency partly satisfied this desire by evaluating effort in terms of busy-ness. But the busy-ness standard produced its own problems. It might be carried to a ludicrous extreme, as it seemed to be when counselors were discouraged from talking with one another.[15] But the more significant problem was that, despite the failure of an occasional counselor on this score, the standard was too easily satisfied. When most or all of the counselors kept busy, there was little basis for differential evaluation. When contracts were lost, somebody had to be laid off, and the formalized standards for job evaluation were inadequate in making layoff decisions. In such situations, more subtle and personal standards came into play. Counselors usually did not know what the operative standards were. They might learn some of them, as we saw in the case of Counselor F and her supervisor. But those who were told what their failures were— for example, the counselor who clowned around—were encouraged to believe that the agency would be patient with them. When layoffs were necessary, they learned what their "score" was, but too late. Up to that point, their retention on staff led to uncertainty over work standards among other counselors. Even when the "non-productive" counselors were laid off, there was no certainty as to why they were laid off.[16] The only certainty was that their layoffs were not based on their being assigned to the canceled program—since "contract lines are crossed."[17] That is, the least productive counselors were released even if not assigned to the canceled program.

Uncertainty, induced by the precarious fiscal situation of the agency and by vague and personal standards of performance, appeared to be the dominant means of control and discipline exercised by the agency. Making placements was one means of performing satisfactorily, but as one counselor reported, that was not enough: Supervisors expected more without always clearly specifying what it was. As the agency became more dependent upon contracts and as the contracts themselves became less secure, the uncertainty of who would be laid off in the event of contract loss discouraged counselors from "making waves" and encouraged them to "keep busy."

Thus, despite the fact that the counselors were not systematically evaluated on the basis of their placement statistics, they acted as if they were, weeding out the clients who would be hard to place. For those clients who were not weeded out at YEA, there was no displacement of the organizational goal of job placement. However, there was an important change in the clientele and a subversion of the purposes of all parties. It is understandable that Blau could conclude that despite the displacement of goals, the introduction of performance records improved placement operations considerably. The same observation might be made with regard to YEA. However, it seems more important to recognize that improvement in placements was obtained at the cost of sacrificing the clientele. It is ironic that the counselors probably did make a greater effort to serve such clients when the agency was not held fully accountable for its work. The "performance contracts" may have contributed to the neglect of the primary "target population" for which such contracts were funded in the first place.[18]

The weeding out of certain clients bore some resemblance to the goal displacement described by Blau, but there was even more resemblance to the phenomenon of "creaming" described by others. "Creaming" refers to the practice of serving the most qualified clients rather than the most disadvantaged ones because the payoff is more certain. The main difference is that the weeding out of certain undesirable clients is the process by which the creaming is accomplished.

At the cost of losing our focus on YEA temporarily, we can examine this process in other CETA-funded agencies, hoping to gain not only a useful comparison and a somewhat broader framework for the findings at YEA, but some new insights into the mechanisms of the CETA program that contribute to the elimination of clients who are not easily serviced.

THE MANPOWER PROGRAM IN OTHER AGENCIES

The CETA program, the reader may recall, was enacted in 1973, with the intention of consolidating the various manpower programs in existence at the time, decentralizing the planning and administration of the manpower program, and decategorizing the federal manpower funds so they did not come already committed to certain target groups. The program was modified several times in the 1974–78 period: A new public-service-employment component was added, for example, as was a new youth program—the Youth Employment and Demonstration Projects Act of 1977. Title I of the act remained essentially unchanged, however. Title I was viewed as the main title under which decentralized and decategorized services would be provided, and it covered the full range of training and other services related to employment: classroom and on-the-job training, work experience, public-service employment, basic and remedial education, training allowances, counseling and orientation, and so forth. Under Title I the prime sponsors were given the authority to design their programs, deciding how the programs would be implemented and who would be served.

The prime sponsors were the 451 political jurisdictions around the country that contracted with the Department of Labor. These prime sponsors were often cities (of 100,000 population or more), but some prime sponsors were counties, either singly or together with other counties in a consortium; still other prime sponsors (or "primes," as DOL officials often called them) were "balance of state" units (everything left over after the urban primes were designated). It was the prime sponsors and their responsibilities that gave CETA its decentralized structure. In YEA's case, the prime sponsor was Central City—specifically, its manpower department. Prime sponsors did not necessarily perform all manpower services, as the reader is well aware of now. The actual delivery of services was often farmed out to "subgrantees" like YEA, many of whom were in the manpower business before CETA came into being.

In 1978, the CETA program required a new authorization by Congress if it was not to expire, calling for a close scrutiny of the program. One of the congressional committees in whose jurisdiction this lay was the Manpower and Housing subcommittee of the House Committee on Government Operations. This subcommittee, chaired by Rep. Cardiss Collins of Illinois, conducted eight days of hearings spread over several months and held in various cities across the country. The focus of these particular hearings was "how well the hard-core unemployed are being assisted by these programs, and the effectiveness of the Labor Department monitoring of and assistance to prime sponsors," according to the committee chairperson.

One day of the hearings was devoted to the problems of community-based organizations (CBOs) such as the National Urban League (NUL) and the Opportunities Industrialization Center (OIC) network, which participated in CETA as service deliverers (subgrantees) to prime sponsors. The record of these hearings was printed for use of the Committee on Government Operations under the title "Department of Labor Monitoring of Manpower Programs for the Hard to Employ." The briefest possible summary of the CBO hearings would be to say that after allowing for certain special problems of these large national organizations, the comments of their officials paralleled the findings reported here for YEA.

At YEA, we recall, the increasing dependence of the agency on government funding, coupled with the greater specificity of performance in its CETA contracts (monthly quotas of placements, for example), was seen to be associated with the weeding out of clients who would be hard to place on jobs (the very clients the agency was intended to serve) by deceptive statistical reports and by serious consideration of a new mission (actually, a new and different type of service) by the agency's board of trustees. Thus, the agency was soon serving its traditional clientele less effectively, while the board was becoming frustrated by the CETA contract restrictions, disturbed by the way the DOL seemed to be running the agency, and perhaps no longer finding the task of job placement for its clientele as challenging as it once was.

We cannot measure the dependence of the CBOs involved as accurately as we did for YEA. But the testimony does provide ample evidence of the amount of federal money involved and the scale of the operations that depended on it. OIC, for example, was described by its executive director as having 140 programs operating in 48 states. "This morning we have some 50,000 trainees that are in classes. We have over 6,000 staff people." There is no direct evidence on the amount of federal money that went to OIC annually or what proportion of its total income this represented. Although desirable, the information is not crucial here. We know that, in the words of its founder, it went from operating in 1964 "in a $1 a year leased jailhouse owned by the City of Philadelphia" to the scale of operations described above, financed by federal funds—first the Manpower Development and Training Act (MDTA), as well as other sources, then CETA.

Like YEA (and the Urban League), OIC is a mission-oriented organization. The mission of OIC, expressed by its founder, included the following objectives: "To foster and nurture a sense of self-pride which will give the trainee confidence in himself and enable him to participate with dignity in the total society . . . . To stimulate loyalty and pride in the community . . . a sense of brotherhood . . . . To develop an awareness of man's relationships and responsibilities to his fellow man . . . . "

Both OIC and NUL had Washington offices to handle relations with the DOL and Congress. The deputy director of the Urban League's Washington bureau briefed the House committee on the organization's manpower program and the long-standing mission of the Urban League.

Presently, the National Urban League, Inc., headquartered in New York City, consists of four regional offices and 110 affiliates located in 35 states . . . . Our involvement with manpower programming did not begin with the enactment of CETA. The initial focus on employment and its impact on Black freedmen and women had its genesis in the creation of such organizations as the Association for the Protection of Colored Women, formed in 1905; the Committee for Improving the Industrial Conditions of Negroes in New York, formed in 1906 . . . and the Committee on Urban Conditions Among Negroes formed in 1910. From an amalgamation of these organizations in 1911 the National League on Urban Conditions Among Negroes emerged . . . later shortened to the National Urban League . . . . In 1968, the National Urban League's on-the-job training program . . . was created. That program changed its focus in 1973 with the advent of CETA, and shifted from a national job training program to an overall technical assistance project funded by the Department of Labor . . . . One hundred Urban League affiliates currently operate CETA programs totaling over 42 million dollars.

Elsewhere it is revealed that the Urban League affiliates operated "251 various programs" at that time, serving about 50,000 clients a year.

Like YEA, then, OIC and the NUL are mission-oriented organizations and are dependent on federal contracts for a substantial part of their income. Moreover, despite the greater size and national reputations of OIC and the Urban League, they were subject to the same standards for performance assessment in their contracts, particularly placement rates and cost per placement. What was their reaction to the contract constraints? How did the standards affect their selection of clients, and how consistent were they with the mission of the organization?

The associate director of the Urban League's Office of Program Development and Training testified:

One of the major concerns is the Department of Labor's perception—tunnel vision from our viewpoint—of how to measure the success or failure of a program. DOL seems to strictly look at such criteria as the number of persons placed in unsubsidized employment, the salary after training and pre/post training salary differentials. In many cases, these indices cannot adequately measure the value of specific kinds of services being provided by individual programs in particular cities.

A program development specialist from one of the Urban League's regional offices, after first complaining about the relationship between a League affiliate and a local prime sponsor, continued:

Of far greater concern, however, is the impact that present criteria for program evaluation has on the ability of programs to fully address the needs of the long-term unemployed who may encounter multiple barriers to employment . . . . Presently, the primary consideration of prime sponsors when they attempt to assess the effectiveness of program delivery agents continues to focus on cost per placement . . . . The heavy emphasis on cost per placement has . . . been used by prime sponsors as the rationale for excluding programs designed to serve the most critically unemployed. Such an emphasis results in the practice of creaming. We hope that the proposed targeting provisions of the re-enactment [of CETA] would ease the problem. In the interim, however, prime sponsors continue to shun anything more than lip service to programs providing intensive service for long-term unemployed clients [and] the majority of prime sponsors believe that only the "bottom line", placement, matters to the Department of Labor.

As we saw at YEA, the time and effort spent on marginal clients may well be wasted, since they may not be placed on jobs—which is the "bottom line" (or one of them) referred to above. The weeding out of such clients is part of the process of creaming.

Finally (as far as the Urban League is concerned), the OJT director for one of the League's West Coast affiliates had this to say:

Basically, one of the key concerns I have is that the CETA system is not designed to serve those who are really in need—those who we consider the really hardcore unemployed individuals. The main reason for that is that the year-to-year funding places a severe handicap on the program's ability to address the long-term problems of individuals . . . . In addition, in order to serve those who are truly most in need, there must be more money in the area of supportive services so that the individual can survive during the time in which he is involved in the program.

On this point, the Urban League official added that the performance standards must be changed "away from just strict cost-effectiveness" so that "efforts in the area of counseling, motivational training," and so on, could be assessed.

Perhaps it is appropriate to note here that the CBOs such as the Urban League and OIC regarded themselves, with some justification, as the experts on manpower training for disadvantaged clients. Members of the committee also shared this opinion. Being "minority organizations," the CBOs felt themselves better equipped to understand the needs of the populations the programs were designed to serve. One of their most frequent complaints during the hearings was that the Department of Labor and the prime sponsors ignored their expertise, did not call on them for advice, and often sought to exclude them from the planning process. The DOL, on the other hand, seemed desirous of standardizing and mass-producing the techniques developed by the CBOs—the major ones of which, at least, were all equally effective, but whose effectiveness was in part based on recruiting and concentrating on those clients who responded favorably to their techniques and ideologies.

"Of the groups we have talked with to date, perhaps the CBOs can make the strongest claim that they seek out the hard to employ," the chairperson of the committee stated at the outset of that day's hearing. "They have had considerable experience in dealing with people who had lost faith in their ability to compete in the economic system. They have devised approaches designed to renew the client's sense of . . . self-worth, to motivate them for training, and to instill in them the attributes necessary for success in the world of work."

OIC, in particular, was praised for its work by another member of the committee:

First of all, I would like to express appreciation to these gentlemen for coming to testify. Dr. Sullivan [founder of OIC] has long been known to us in Pennsylvania. We know of the good job he has done there, and now it is spread throughout the nation. I think this subcommittee has to listen very carefully to the things you have to say, because your record has been one of success long before we had CETA programs and other government efforts headed in the direction you've been going for some time.

The DOL was not listening to what OIC had to say, apparently, to judge from the testimony of its executive director:

The employment and training system seems to have changed after 1968. The emphasis shifted to developing an administrative framework and less on ways to serve the unemployed . . . . OIC has learned a great deal about ways to serve the unemployed. Unfortunately, these learnings are secondary to administrative neatness. The DOL is more concerned with eliminating duplication than discovering which agency in our community can provide the best service to certain groups of people . . . . In my view, the language of CETA establishes a legitimate role for all CBOs. This has not yet been implemented by DOL.

Ironically, the CBOs, which claim to represent local populations but which are also national organizations with their own standard techniques and philosophies, found themselves in opposition to the local prime sponsors quite often. These CBOs have strong support in Congress and in many ways are more comfortable with a national program than a decentralized one, although as we have noted they chafe at the performance standards imposed on them by the DOL because the uniform, simplistic standards encourage creaming rather than effective and comprehensive service.

At one point in the hearing, the staff director of the committee asked an OIC official:

"Is it true that in Washington for a time you ran a program without stipends . . . and you were able to fill your classes even though you were competing with other programs that did pay stipends?"

"That is right. We had a waiting list of over 2,500 people."

"Why would he choose to go to OIC in a case like that?" [the committee chair asked].

"He knew that OIC, after he had completed training, was going to put him in a job that was unsubsidized. We had a relationship with over 400 employers in the Washington area who would hire our people because they realized that they were willing to help themselves. They were not coming to us just for the stipend."

OIC was eager to lower the cost-per-placement even further by greatly reducing or eliminating the allowances trainees received while in the program. For many CBOs, allowances were seen as necessary to enable clients to remain in programs while being prepared for employment. In OIC, however, allowances were seen as "handouts" which mitigated the effect of their appeals to self-help and pride. What OIC particularly objected to was that they *had to pay allowances* to get program contracts from local prime sponsors, even though the allowances were not desired and were thought to be counterproductive. It appeared that the allowances prevented OIC from creaming for the kind of trainee who responded to its particular appeal—an unusual twist to the problem. Here is the explanation of this approach, offered by OIC's executive director:

Our motto, as mandated by Dr. Sullivan, is that we help ourselves. We are not interested in handouts, but we are interested in handups. We have found that folk appreciate more the skills they acquire when there is a little sacrifice—when they have worked for it . . . . The result of the sacrifice is the psychological effect that they have overcome the struggle . . . . This opportunity is denied when we are mandated to pay allowances—in many instances we cannot get contracts with prime sponsors unless we do that. So it is important to us that we maintain the self-help philosophy and do it our way.

Thus, the mandated allowances undermined the mission (and the key selling point) of OIC: to develop strength in its clients through a self-help philosophy.

The assessment of CETA by OIC and NUL officials, although consistent with our own findings at the Youth Employment Agency, has one potential bias: the two organizations were CETA program operators and the views of their officials may have been shaped by the interests of the organizations in some way. CETA was not extensively studied by outsiders, possibly because it was not around long enough, but there are some sources we can draw on.

The DOL commissioned a study of the CETA program in Massachusetts. This was published in 1978 as R & D Monograph 57, "The Implementation of CETA in Eastern Massachusetts and Boston." The study was conducted over a three-year period by scholars of MIT and Northeastern University, with one group studying Boston and the other group studying the program in the eastern part of the state. One of the principal findings of both groups was that the short-term performance indicators used by the DOL in its monitoring of prime sponsor performance, such as the cost-per-placement figure, made no distinction "between the Prime Sponsor which 'creams' clients for training programs and the one which is serving the most disadvantaged."

There was "great pressure on the Prime Sponsor to 'perform' in a manner that will please the DOL," the authors of the eastern Massachusetts study noted, and the main way the DOL graded the prime sponsors was "through the use of short-term performance indicators." There were a great many problems with the performance indicators developed by the DOL:

For example, an indicator called cost-per-placement cannot be appropriately compared across Prime Sponsors, as one may be "creaming" clients and another serving the most disadvantaged. Further, the same . . . figure tells nothing about the length of time the "placed" person remained on the job, nor does it offer any hint of the fate of fellow participants who were not placed. The latter may have returned to formal schooling or gone on to another program— outcomes which are not necessarily negative. Finally, comparison of the cost-per-placement across local Prime Sponsors, the state, region, or nation is inappropriate, since economic conditions, comprehensiveness of support services and the like may differ drastically. These three obvious limitations of the most widely quoted short-term performance indicators illustrate that it, at best, should only be utilized as a "flag" to point out areas where attention might be needed and not offered as evidence of a good or a poor program. To a certain extent, all of the short-term performance indicators suffer from definitional and contextual limitations.

At YEA, of course, we were not so interested in how these indicators were limited for research purposes as we were in how the indicators themselves structured, even distorted, the program—encouraging the use of temporary jobs, for example, so as to record a placement, and of course weeding out the hardest to place clients so as to maintain a favorable placement rate and cost per placement.

The authors of the Boston study also noted that "two criteria have predominated," with one of them being "placement in an unsubsidized job, at a wage above a specified level." As a result, the focus of the program was on the short-term outcome: "Being hired and working one day constitutes a job placement." It was recommended that "extra credit" (and resources, presumably) be given for placing those with exceptional labor-market handicaps such as educational level, minority status, age, physical handicaps, emotional problems, and language and cultural barriers. This would be a "disincentive for creaming," in the authors' view, and by this means "the selection of candidates would be more open and more objective" rather than being governed exclusively by their prospects for immediate placement. We might note, by the way, that YEA's clients often had two additional handicaps not listed above: drug addiction and correctional history.

One other factor was cited by the authors in explaining the extremely short-range focus of the Boston program, and this was the practice of funding programs for one year.

One year contracts encourage shortrun goals and shortrun tactics, not longrun planning and longrun strategy. They also encourage shortrun programs that are likely to lead to placements in jobs with few promotion opportunities. A big step in the direction of longer range planning would be to fund agencies . . . longer than 12 months . . . . Such programs should be open-ended to permit adjustment to changing labor market conditions.

In 1976 the National Commission for Manpower Policy held three regional conferences for the purpose of assessing the national manpower policy. Participants included prime sponsors, federal officials, CBOs, academics, and others. The views expressed at the conferences were published by the commission in December 1976 under the title "Directions for a National Manpower Policy: A Report on the Proceedings of Three Regional Conferences" (Special Report No. 13). The proceedings of the western regional conference show that the topic of accountability "was raised repeatedly by the participants." There was no disagreement about the need to develop a system of accountability, it was reported. However, "concerns were expressed over the problems of establishing performance standards. There was apparent consensus that any such procedure and related performance standards should be developed in consultation with prime sponsors and that standards utilized should recognize local variation in population characteristics and labor market problems."

The author of one background paper prepared for the conference concluded that national performance guidelines "work against the development of innovative programs of service to welfare recipients, ex-offenders, drug abusers or other hard-to-serve groups" and documented a case for a more efficient multiyear funding to avoid "planning hastily to crisis after crisis." The author of another paper observed that "more flexibility, not less, is needed if localities are to discover how to be effective in helping those with minimal skills."

The chairman of the National Commission for Manpower Policy, testifying before the House Manpower and Housing subcommittee, described the situation in this way: "We now have a system of rewarding the prime sponsor . . . for being happy with their performance . . . in terms of this numbers game. You have to add another dimension to the numbers game, which is a quality outcome." What was needed, he suggested, was a way of telling the prime sponsors that "it is better for them to serve 50 people, 35 of whom make it to regular employment, than to serve 100 people, of whom only 10 get into regular employment. Otherwise, they will not do it."

It seems that virtually everyone involved in CETA, from the DOL down to program operators, agreed that the performance standards and the short-term funding contributed to the creaming of clients and de-flection of the program away from some of its main objectives. There is no reason to question this. The conclusion was based on extensive experience involving many programs, and the same thing, in the form of weeding out the target population, was found at YEA. However, there was surprisingly little attempt made in the congressional hearings and in the various DOL-sponsored studies and conferences to document the assertion.

What evidence is there that the practices described resulted in the weeding out (or conversely, the creaming) of clients? The detailed view of this process in other agencies, as we have described it at YEA, is not available. However, we can compare client characteristics in other pro-grams prior to and during CETA, to see if there were any changes and if some of the same factors were involved. We may recall that at YEA, age, work experience, and education were important factors in getting a job and thus in weeding out clients. That is, younger, less educated, and less experienced clients were weeded out.

The Boston study, cited above, shows some tendency in the direc-tion of weeding out less-educated clients. Despite some limitations in the data used, 18.5 percent of clients in the pre-CETA manpower pro-gram in Boston (1972–73) had an 8th-grade education or less, while in the CETA program this figure dropped to 11.1 percent. At the same time, those with some education beyond high school rose from 2.4 per-cent to 11.4 percent. That is, the pre-CETA program had a greater pro-portion of clients with minimal education and fewer clients with an ed-ucation beyond the high school level.

Mirengoff and Rindler (1978) studied a sample of 28 prime sponsors in the CETA program and, among other things, compared the age, ed-ucation, and economic status of pre-CETA and CETA clients. Exact comparisons are not possible because programs shift from one category to another. In general, however, the authors concluded that a compar-ison of the characteristics of CETA participants with a composite of en-rollees in categorical manpower programs in fiscal year 1974, prior to CETA, showed a shift toward older clients. Although youth were still in the majority in CETA Title I programs, the proportion of younger (and harder to place) clients was declining. Prior to CETA, 63 percent of the clients in a combination of programs (including the Neighbor-hood Youth Corps in-school program) were 22 years old or younger. By 1977, Title I programs were down to 51 percent with respect to the same age category. For those 18 and under, the shift was from 46 per-cent to 31 percent. The same trend was evident in educational attain-ment: The proportion of clients with 12 or more years of schooling went from 34 percent to 50 percent in the same period of time. "Pressure on local sponsors to meet goals, competition among program operators

for contracts, and emphasis on performance evaluation encourage selection of the applicants most likely to succeed," the authors observed.
"These pressures are reinforced by the difficulty in finding jobs for
manpower trainees who compete with better qualified candidates in a
loose labor market. Program operators prefer trainees who have some
chance of being placed rather than those whose employability is minimal."

In 1976, about 9 percent of the Title I clients in the author's sample
were "direct placements," that is, clients who were placed on jobs
quickly, with no services being provided other than intake, assessment, and job referral. They attributed this to the pressure put on
sponsors to meet the placement quotas and cost estimates. The result
was that program operators gave less attention to the task of preparing
the more disadvantaged clients for employment. Instead, the recruitment of job-ready clients and the use of low-wage, unstable jobs were
encouraged.

Moreover, the authors argue, the quantitative measures used did not
allow an assessment of certain important program benefits such as the
extent to which the number of options available to enrollees was increased, the gains that were derived from the training and work experience programs, how effective the counseling and other supportive
services were, and how successful the programs were in reaching their
target populations.

The effect on programs did not begin in the performance-evaluation
phase, however. Program applications were judged according to whether
or not certain acceptable outcomes and standards were incorporated as
objectives. Mirengoff and Rindler note that the DOL issued guidelines
for reviewing grant applications. The guidelines were meant to be used
flexibly but were subsequently criticized by prime sponsors and program operators because (1) they represented broad averages that were
not applicable to individual areas, especially since there was wide variation in program contents, (2) they did not include certain important
goals that were difficult to quantify such as job stability, and (3) the
guidelines tended to favor programs that produced immediate placement rather than increasing the employability of clients.

The grant review process was described by a regional administrator
of the DOL appearing before the House subcommittee on Manpower
and Housing in 1978, the same hearings that were referred to earlier.

The best way for us to get a grant in the regional office that is an appropriate
grant is to provide in advance the technical assistance and training to the sponsor, to convey to them what kind of grant it is we like to see come in the regional office. We, in developing the grant, try to do that. We conduct a training
session with the sponsors to tell them what it is we would like to see in the

grant application when it is received . . . . One of the things we are most interested in . . . is *who is being served* . . . . Another question that we get involved in very seriously in the grant review and approval process is *how to do it*. [Emphasis added.]

The committee chairperson later asked the regional administrator if the system of reporting required of prime sponsors, based on the objectives and criteria built into the grants, provided "opportunities and encouragement to prime sponsors who want to actually reach the hard to employ." He replied:

That is a very difficult question . . . . When a sponsor has a proposal for that kind of a program, the sponsor needs to be very clear in their grant application to us. Why this particular program is different, whey they are choosing to expend additional money on training people who are harder to employ than average . . . that kind of proposal will be approved. On the other hand, I just looked yesterday at my total CETA budget in this region . . . and we are approaching $2 billion. Now, managing something of this size, we need to be able to deal in some kind of aggregate. In aggregate, the general rule is: lower that cost for employment.

The administrator was asked a little later: What types of goals must the prime sponsors set when they address the problems of the hard to employ? He replied:

Getting that person into employment, that really is our first and most important goal. I think a second area, or a subsequent goal is that the individual at least complete the training that was prescribed. Maybe it is possible to get a placement right away. Clearly, the first objective is achieving the placement; the second objective is completing the training.

Thus, not only were the grant applications framed in terms of objectives and performance standards that were "acceptable" to the DOL but, as we have noted repeatedly, the performance of the prime sponsors and program operators was, in the end, assessed according to how well they met these targets, and renewal of the grant or contract was based on this evaluation. Even that arrangement, as structured as it was, might have left some room for innovation and flexibility during the life of the grant. But the DOL took steps (unintentionally, perhaps) to close that opening as well.

One of the department's responsibilities was to provide technical assistance to the prime sponsors. Technical assistance was defined in terms of helping sponsors improve their ability to meet the objectives of the legislation using the department's own expertise and disseminating the successful results of other programs. The technical assistance role of the

DOL might have infused the entire program with more of an innovative and experimental spirit if it had not been combined with the monitoring role.

The same federal employee was charged with monitoring a contract and also providing technical assistance to the sponsor. This combination was often criticized by the prime sponsors during the House committee hearings in 1978. One, for example, complained: "You know, it is just such an obvious contradiction. I am not going to call the regional office to say that I am having trouble in supported work and have somebody who can write a letter . . . coming out and saying that I need corrective action in these areas." The CBOs were more likely to be critical of interference from the prime sponsors rather than from the DOL; in their view they were quite capable of providing technical assistance rather than needing it, and they had their own "national programs" that were monitored locally. Despite this, the effect was the same inasmuch as the prime sponsors were monitoring on the basis of the federal standards. "We monitor the monitors" was how one regional DOL administrator described the department's role in monitoring the CBOs and other program operators.

The chairman of the National Commission for Manpower Policy discussed the problem during his testimony before the House committee:

It is a very awkward relationship. If the regional representative of the Department of Labor is a sort of local monitor, then it is very difficult for the prime sponsor staff to open up and admit what their difficulties are. It is a game in which the prime sponsors try to keep the Federal officials as uninformed about their business as possible.

However, the combination of roles was defended by a regional administrator for DOL, at the same hearing, in these words:

Another issue which always surfaces in terms of our management responsibilities in the regional office is the combination . . . of both the monitoring and the technical assistant role. It is essentially a black-hat white-hat kind of situation. The question is often asked: Can the Federal representative who one day has to go out and tell the sponsors, "You are doing this, this, and this wrong," can that same person go out and be helpful, a technical assistance provider, not threatening, and get ideas accepted? That is a very difficult role to achieve. On the other hand . . . I feel it is the best way to do things. I firmly feel that it is important to be not only a problem-finder, but a problem-fixer.

To some extent the Department of Labor was undoubtedly caught in a game that it had no choice but to play. The deputy director of the National Commission for Manpower Policy pointed out (in "CETA: An

Analysis of the Issues") that the CETA legislation required the secretary of labor to collect certain information:

The law states that information shall be collected on:

1. enrollee characteristics, including age, sex, race, health, education level, and previous wage and employment experience;
2. duration in training and employment situations . . . ; and
3. total dollar cost per trainee, including breakdown between salary or stipend, training and supportive services, and administrative services.

As currently organized, he added, the CETA information system had only "a specified minimum standard data base" rather than a uniform reporting system—the original intent of which was "to collect the DOL information without imposing undue restrictions on the decentralized system." Of course, in the absence of any other word, the minimum standard data base came to be the operating standards for the program and the basis of program evaluation.

There were other political factors that were not entirely (if at all) in the DOL's control. The Office of Management and Budget (OMB), for example, appeared to have a say in what forms the DOL used and thus in the kinds of performance data that would be available for evaluation of prime sponsors and subgrantees. Testifying before the House oversight committee, a DOL official described the role of the OMB in this regard. "There is a standard reporting system," he said, "and every single prime sponsor reports certain items. I think every single one of us has a problem with the reporting system that we currently use. It captures some information we like; it doesn't capture the kind of information you were talking about which might be useful," he added, responding to one of the committee members. There is a standard national form? he was asked. "Yes," he replied. "That is all we are allowed to impose on the prime sponsors." So you can't do more or less than that? the congressman continued. "No," the DOL official replied, "unless OMB were to authorize a change in the standard reporting system that is used across the country."

Then, too, there is undoubtedly an inherent conflict—even a contradiction—in the structure of a federalized system, between federal and local officials. In this case, DOL is drawn in on the side of the federal establishment since that is where its own interests and its own accountability to Congress lie. In this view, it would be unrealistic to expect the DOL to see things from the locals' perspective, though no harmful intent or incompetence would be implied. CETA, in particular, was a contradictory piece of legislation. The chairperson of the House oversight committee noted the first day of the hearings:

The second area we have selected for examination is the effectiveness of the Department of Labor's monitoring and support of the over–400 prime sponsors who administer the CETA programs. The relationship here shares the problems and promise common to other federally funded efforts administered by state and local governments. Local knowledge of conditions permits programs to be fine-tuned, but the Federal Government's discharge of its responsibilities to the taxpayers requires that it assure that the money is spent efficiently and in accordance with the law.

This was only the first of many occasions when this theme was stated, the implication being that DOL chiefs had the impossible task of somehow devising a manageable and effective program involving officials at the federal and local levels who are always to some extent suspicious of each other and reluctant to concede any power to the other.

Whatever the reason for the DOL's insistence on national performance standards in the CETA program—standards that, as we have frequently pointed out, hampered the program in a number of ways—we cannot attribute it entirely to being a victim of uncontrollable factors, however. Despite many problems and much advice the DOL did not see the distinction between minimum standards and program requirements—based on local conditions—or else took no action to deal with the matter. And, of course, it was the DOL that dictated the contents of program grants and that offered technical assistance through its monitors, rather like offering legal advice through the police department. In short, the department consistently resolved the program's contradictions in favor of greater standardization, uniformity, control, and quantitative measurement. "Would anyone seriously argue that placement is a *final* objective of CETA expenditures—to be distinguished from placement as an *intermediate* step in improving enrollee well-being?" asked the author of one background paper prepared for the National Commission for Manpower Policy (NCMP) and published as part of "CETA: An Analysis of the Issues."

Apparently many did so argue—at least by the force of their decisions. And they were not limited to the DOL and its staff. The upper echelon of the NCMP itself—the leading manpower advisory group in the federal government—could not, in the end, come down on the side of the substantive *objectives* of CETA as opposed to the political interests involved. The executive director of the NCMP wrote in the publication cited above that "a more sensible approach [in making program decisions] might be to allow service deliverers to make these decisions on the basis of their own experiences and insights." There would still be a need to evaluate outcomes at both the local and national levels, she added, but "it would not be necessary to prejudge or prespecify the way they are to be achieved. This approach is, of course, at the core of a decentralized and decategorized manpower system." However, there is almost no chance of its coming to pass if the view expressed elsewhere by the same official prevailed: " . . . if one believes that objectives can be clarified, *that federal priorities must prevail where federal dollars are at stake* and that a reasonably sophisticated set of performance standards can be designed, then the above problems need not be viewed as insurmountable" (emphasis added). However, unless federal priorities happen to coincide with the priorities in all the local areas (most unlikely, we would suppose), the problems of a decentralized program will remain very difficult ones, even if not insurmountable. When there is a conflict, the federal dollars and the priorities defined in Washington will take precedence.

So often were the contradictions of CETA stated, without noting their opposition, that it must be wondered if the manpower establishment ever conceived of the problem as one involving a contradiction. The chairman of NCMP in his *Third Annual Report* (May 1978) to the president and Congress noted (p. 3) that "the Commission strongly holds that the principal thrust of the CETA program should be to enhance the employability of structurally unemployed persons. This means that such individuals, as a result of their participation in a CETA program, should have improved prospects for getting and holding regular jobs at higher earnings."

But how is it to be determined if prime sponsors and program operators are serving this purpose? Elsewhere in the report, the same official says: "The Commission strongly believes that the major emphasis on the development of performance standards should be in terms of output measures, such as increased employment and higher earnings."

All the findings, without exception, suggest that such standardized quantitative criteria, when combined with short-term funding, will result in the elimination of certain clients from the program. Granted that some assessment of such a program is necessary and desirable, it must be recognized that "employment" (placements) and "earnings increases" will be unattainable for some in the short run. Specifying them as performance requirements will simply stack the deck against the ones needing preparatory and supportive services. In a curious way, the very purpose of CETA—to improve the "prospects for getting and holding regular jobs at higher earnings—when stated as a performance standard and measured, results in the withdrawal of services for the group ("structurally unemployed persons") for whom the purpose was stated.

CETA was intended to be a *decentralized* but *coordinated* manpower program, with the coordination being done by federal officials, of course. It would appear that a merely decentralized program, with genuine local planning and administration, would be workable, even if not likely to come to pass and even if it might bring in its wake its own problems. Or a national program that was designed to be coordinated could work very well in certain respects. But a decentralized *and* coordinated manpower program, such as CETA was designed to be, will be ineffective unless the coordination and evaluation is sufficiently loose to permit some flexibility and adaptation to the conditions encountered in various areas by different programs working with different clienteles. CETA was, in this sense, only "coordinated." But, again ironically, mere coordination in a decentralized program is insufficient, because while everything is coordinated, nothing really gets done. CETA will be seen as just another liberal program that did not work if we fail to carefully examine what it did and did not do, and why. We cannot do full justice to that here, except as it affected YEA, our principal subject.

CETA did not increase the autonomy of YEA, and it did not increase the overall effectiveness of YEA in dealing with a very "disadvantaged" group of clients. There were greater resources, but the contracts and the monitoring tended to force out the most disadvantaged for the sake of placements. Since serving a disadvantaged population requires first of all engaging them, maintaining contact with them, and making an effort on their behalf, it is in this sense that we conclude that the new approach to manpower incorporated in CETA did not increase YEA's overall effectiveness.

What CETA *did* do at YEA was give the counselors and others a sense of having at last some of the tools needed to do their work. We have not stressed this enough here. This may have been its major accomplishment. Unfortunately, however, it may have been negated by the monitoring process, by the terms of accountability and the other factors discussed. And, of course, it did more than provide counselors with a *sense* of having tools to work with. They were actually used: skills-training vouchers and remedial education, for example. This was not the focus of our study; it would have been more of a systematic evaluation if so. The fact that we came to focus more on how the structure and processes of CETA to some extent negated the purposes of the program should not be taken to mean that nothing of a positive nature was accomplished. *Too little* was accomplished, without a doubt. But this assessment must be seen alongside the enormity of the task, and the new and changing expectations of manpower programs. We expect them to progress, to do better—no program can ever do enough. In fact, the gap may *widen*. And the particular innovations in CETA, especially local planning and supervision of programs, induced very high expectations.

In the end we can only say that the problems that others—prime sponsors and CBOs—had with CETA were similar to the problems observed at YEA. The impact of the CETA program on YEA had much to do with a new type of contract (new, that is, for YEA in its relations with government agencies) that incorporated very specific and unchanging performance criteria that were not easily attainable for many of the agency's clients at the time.

NOTES

1. *New York Times,* December 26, 1972.

2. One client was over 20 and was referred to another agency, in keeping with the agency's new policy of serving only clients who had not reached their twentieth birthday.

3. This information was gathered and reported by one of the counselors.

4. Peter Blau, *The Dynamics of Bureaucracy,* 3d ed. (Chicago: University of Chicago Press, 1963), p. 6. There is the possibility that the public agency studied by Blau may have virtually eliminated the altruistic type from consideration through its hiring standards (presumably based on examinations stressing "intellectual" qualities). This would lead to entirely different observations.

5. Ibid., p. 39.

6. Ibid., p. 40.

7. Ibid., p. 41.

8. Ibid., p. 43.

9. Blau does not employ the distinction of "real goals" used by Perrow and others in separating professed goals from ones that are operationalized. Blau's findings of "goal displacement" is, in a sense, partly due to his failure to distinguish between the real goals and the professed goals of the agency he studied.

10. It would be interesting to discuss the "functions" and the "dysfunctions" that Blau presents as examples of contradictions. For example, the contradiction involved in the supervisors' desire to be free of the necessity of criticizing subordinates and their resistance to their "clerk" status when they are so freed. But it is extraneous here.

11. The conclusion that the practice of weeding out clients was known to the director is based on his statements to me as to what the counselors did. This included the assertion that counselors were supposed to motivate the clients to return to the agency.

12. The council was composed of five members; three were laid off within the next two months. (Two of them were laid off four days after this meeting took place.) Counselor G and Counselor J were on the council and were still on staff in June 1977.

13. From what is known about goal displacement and the fallacy of the "single criterion," this reluctance may have many things to recommend it, though we must note the problems it causes with respect to uncertainty and ambiguity.

14. In any event, it is difficult to comprehend what might be meant by "good rapport." The observations of counselors working indicated that most counselors employed a rather direct and didactic style.

15. Counselors' talking with job developers did not seem to be viewed in the same way: There was legitimate reason for them to talk about job require-

ments, employer quirks, and so forth. But counselors did not need to talk to other counselors; their work was seen as independent. We note that the annual evaluations rate *independent decision-making,* and not *consulting with colleagues.*

16. Perhaps we can only conclude from this that the problem of standards is an extremely difficult one. No matter which course is chosen, some undesired consequences can be anticipated.

17. If a counselor was assigned to a program that was canceled, he may have been retained (if he was "productive")—while a counselor who was assigned to another program may have been laid off (if he was not considered to be "productive").

18. The performance contracts came along at about the same time that the job market worsened. Thus, both may have been involved in weeding out the target population. This may have been the "ultimate dysfunction."

REFERENCES

The material on CETA in this chapter was drawn from the following sources. The references are alphabetical by title. Where individuals prepared contributions to the publications and they were identified, their names and the titles of their papers are given also.

An Assessment of CETA: Third Annual Report to the President and the Congress of the National Commission for Manpower Policy. Special Report No. 7 of the National Commission for Manpower Policy (NCMP). Washington, D.C.: Government Printing Office, May 1978.

CETA: An Analysis of the Issues. Special Report No. 23 of the NCMP. Washington, D.C.: Government Printing Office, May 1978.

> "Introduction and Summary," by Isabel V. Sawhill (pp. 1–30).
>
> "Program Outcomes," by Bradley Schiller (pp. 105–26).
>
> "Program Information Systems," by Patrick O'Keefe (pp. 185–216).
>
> "Performance Measurement in the CETA System," by David Stevens (pp. 217–41).

CETA: Manpower Programs under Local Control, by William Mirengoff and Lester Rindler. Washington, D.C.: National Academy of Sciences, 1978.

Department of Labor Monitoring of Manpower Programs for the Hard to Employ. Hearings before a subcommittee of the Committee on Government Operations, House of Representatives, 95th Cong. 2d Sess.: April 5, 7, 13, May 2, June 16, July 21, August 17, and September 28, 1978. Washington, D.C.: Government Printing Office, 1979.

Directions for a National Manpower Policy: A Collection of Policy Papers Prepared for Three Regional Conferences. Washington, D.C.: Government Printing Office, 1978. In particular, the following papers were used:

> "CETA: The Basic Assumptions and Future Prospects," by Robert McPherson (pp. 195–214).

"Manpower Programs and Services: The Infrastructure from the Local Perspective," by Eunice Elton (pp. 215–30).

The Implementation of CETA in Eastern Massachusetts and Boston, R & D Monograph 57, U.S. DOL, Employment and Training Administration. Washington, D.C.: Government Printing Office, 1978. The authors of the eastern Massachusetts study were Thomas A. Barrocci and Charles A. Meyers. The authors of the Boston study were Morris Horowitz, Irwin Herrnstadt, and Marlene B. Seltzer.

8

Contracts and Conflict

If the contracts themselves prompted certain changes in YEA—changes adversely affecting the traditional clientele of the agency and thus its mission, as well as the purposes of the contract programs—loss of the contracts (when this occurred) was equally devastating. Morale suffered, and with that, a certain degree of organizational effectiveness was lost. The contract game was a peculiar one that, once begun, could not be ended without paying a heavy penalty.

At a meeting of the executive staff on May 16, 1976, the director reported that the commissioner of the city's Department of Employment had informed him that "the funds for our Ex-Addict contract have been cut." The Juvenile Bureau contract was also lost that year. The junior draftsman program was running its last cycle of trainees (perhaps only temporarily) due to the lack of job openings in engineering and architectural firms.

On May 7, 1976, YEA's director had received a telegram from the Social Agency Employees Union. The telegram said that "the undersigned union represents the majority of your counselors, clerical employees, and job developers" and requested a meeting "for the purpose of discussing terms and conditions of employment."

By May 11, the union was out, rejected by its members in YEA, and a staff representation committee had been elected. On May 12 the committee sent a memo to the staff, announcing the names of those elected to the committee and the committee's plans. The five members elected included the director's administrative assistant.[1] The memo announced that the committee would meet "every Thursday at 4:00 pm" and that "any matter that needs our attention should be made known to any or all members prior to the meeting," and it stated that the "revision of Personnel Practices will be one of the first major projects." The first meeting was scheduled for the following day (May 13): "time will be

devoted to defining our role and making such a committee a permanent part of YEA."

The factors that led to union affiliation in the first place and the events
that led to repudiation of the union were recounted with some uncertainty by the counselors and administrators, especially the latter. No
one seemed able to recall clearly the sequence of events of the May 7–
May 11 period. The confusion (in fact and in memory) may have been
increased by the May 16 notification that the Narcotic Rehabilitation
Agency (NRA) would not be able to renew the addict program. This
was the largest program in the agency, in terms of employment of staff.
The layoffs that resulted from this may have seemed to be part of the
agency's response to the unionization.

The staff was unionized for only four days. One counselor reported
that a few days prior to unionization, the director had taken a group of
staff members out to lunch after he had "found out we were thinking
of going union." The director, she said, had "made it plain that he really
wanted to prevent it and would do everything he could to meet our
demands if we didn't go to the union." When the chairman of the Staff
Grievance Committee returned from lunch, she continued, he recommended to the staff that they "hold off on the union, and try to deal
directly with this ourselves." The staff apparently decided otherwise;
shortly afterwards the director received the telegram from the union
announcing that it represented the workers.

When counselors were asked later what factors had led to the unionization, their responses indicated that in all likelihood only one of the
grievances could have been resolved by a union, a fact that the counselors were not unaware of. One counselor claimed that "many people
were personally motivated because they wanted to make more money."
However, no other counselor advanced this as a reason, and this counselor said that as far as she was concerned, "I don't care about the salary; I make more money than I've ever made." The other counselors
did not believe that salaries as such had been an important issue.

When we examine the interviews, the more important factors behind
the unionization appear to be fear of layoffs, uncertainty over the standards for counselor evaluation, the increasing frustrations of the work
itself, a lack of understanding and concern by the administrators toward the counselors' work problems, and the "total power" of the board
and the administration.

Counselor F said that some "were saying that there was gross inequalities in salaries and favoritism; also, there was a fear of lay-offs."
She added, "The reason I regard unionization with a jaundiced view is
that the things I don't like here are very *personal*, and no union is going
to change them." Many staff members, she said, merely wanted to be
"treated in a different way." Her response to those people had been

that "these are personal things you're talking about," rather than problems appropriate for a union.

Counselor G discounted the problem of salary inequities. "With any job you find that type of complaint," he said. He agreed with Counselor F that the possibility of layoffs and the resulting concern over job security had been important factors. However, he believed that the issue, although an important one, had "developed into nonsense." Some counselors, he said, seemed to think that "once you're on a job, that the job should be yours indefinitely." He added that "in this industry, there's no such thing as job security . . . but people wanted certain changes to be made to guarantee them that job security . . . ."

In Counselor G's view, "the frustration of possible layoffs" was accompanied by "the frustrations of some people feeling that they are not being evaluated on the basis of things they think they *should be* evaluated on." Some counselors, he said, believe that "they should be totally evaluated on the basis of whether they liked kids!"

For Counselor J, the problems leading to unionization might also be summarized under the heading of "frustration," especially that stemming from the administrators' attitude; they were said to be "out of touch" with the counselors' work and "what we really go through," and they were always looking for things to keep the counselors busy despite the pressures they were under. "If they walk around and . . . see you talking to somebody, they will assume you're just fucking up. But in this type of agency . . . you have to stop and talk. You can't continuously, for eight hours, get involved."

This counselor went on to say that he did not mean that "you should be messing around all the time." But, he added, "there's a time when you just have to stop and . . . get your mind off it for a minute." However, when that occurred, "the administrators say, 'I don't think you're seeing enough clients; let's add some more.' " If not that, the counselor said, they would urge him to "do some follow-up" or to get more placements.

The agency had imposed a "total freeze" on salary increases for the past two years, Counselor J said. But the worst part of this had been the attitude of the administration: "a sort of attitude that 'If you don't like it, leave.' " The counselor continued, with considerable anger: "How can you have incentive, if the people you're busting your ass for are turning around and saying, 'If you don't like it, hand in your resignation?' " The counselor claimed that the staff was not expecting "tremendous increases." They would have settled for some compensatory time off or some additional benefits; if nothing else, a "pat on the back and some recognition that you're doing something" would have helped. Instead, he claimed, the administrators "were saying, 'We're doing you a favor; you've got a job.' "

As did the others, this counselor also cited the possibility of lay-offs. "There's been a lot of talk about lay-offs in the social field," he said, "and the first thing you do is run for some type of security." The union "happened to be there in a situation when they needed it." He added that one of the grievances of the staff was that "the personnel practices that we have are backward and archaic; it just gives administration . . . total power in terms of everything, and gives staff really no power." This, the counselor said, was "really insulting to the personnel" because they "could be fired or laid off from this agency without reason at any time" and was for that reason "demoralizing."

By May 24 the director, wielding the board's threat to close the agency rather than accept unionization, had not only broken up the union but forced the new Staff Council to confine its discussions to minor issues. The council acquiesced to the lay-off of staff in accordance with the personnel practices. In the Staff Council's report (to the staff) of a May 24 meeting with the director, success was claimed in getting payday changed to "every other Friday" (rather than the first and the fifteenth of the month), and in having job openings in the agency posted on a bulletin board so that staff members could apply for them. The other two items reported on were acknowledged to be within the prerogatives of the board or the executive director. These reflected two of the prominent complaints expressed by counselors. One involved staff representation at board meetings. The report said that "Mr. G— [president of YEA] will be approached on this when he meets with the Staff." The other concerned layoffs. The report simply listed the various factors considered by the administrators and supervisors in making layoffs and—in the absence of any comment—apparently endorsed them. Seniority was one factor. Job performance ("decided in consultation with supervisors") was the second. The third was the uniqueness of a position, that is, whether it was a "one of a kind" position in the agency. The fourth was "salary line"; it was noted that "economics may determine that a higher paid person cannot be afforded." In addition to these factors, the council said that "the Contract under which a person is employed is an important, if not deciding, factor," and federal "CETA requirements dictate certain racial quotas."

The director's own version of the meeting, which was not distributed to staff, shows that on the payday issue he did "not see any problem" with payday every other Friday. As for the posting of job openings, "it was decided that a staff bulletin board would be set up and job openings posted there." However, the director added that "some supervisors absolutely refuse to have certain people on their staffs, and it is not my policy to push people on supervisors."[2] The director was even more explicit about the staff's (and even his own) tenuous position on the matter of staff representation on the Board. "This is the prerogative of the Board. Everyone, outside of the Board members, attends at the invitation of the Board of Directors. The Board is under no legal obligation to open the meeting to staff and staff has no legal right to insist on this."

The director was asked by one of those present "what his own feelings were on this." He replied that his own feelings "were not relevant." On the issue of who decides layoffs and how, he asserted that "only the Board can approve changes in Personnel Practices" which govern this matter. "Contracts support the bulk of the staff," he noted. "If the source of your salary is removed, you are out—unless the Board chooses to hold on to you."

The layoffs (in late May 1976) following the loss of the addict program were carried out as they had been in the past. Fourteen staff members were laid off. The guiding principle was "getting rid of the dead wood." This did not mean laying off only the leaders of the unionization movement and the subsequent Staff Council. There were too many positions to be eliminated for that, and not all the visible sympathizers were laid off. But the most prominent spokesman for the union was among the victims.

The counselors directed their frustration and resentment toward the board of directors rather than agency administrators in part because the administrators were seen as powerless and ineffective in dealing with the board and often even unable to follow through on their own decisions.

Since the administrators were ineffective and powerless in dealing with the board, they were also ineffective and to some extent powerless in dealing with the staff, even though they possessed the necessary authority. The exercise of authority apparently required a show of some strength or nerve in dealing with the board. When this was not evident, the counselors, in effect, negotiated a truce with the administrators: They refrained from sustained criticism of the administrators' work in exchange for avoidance of "indoctrination" and close supervision of their work.

The administrators were sometimes criticized on a personal level by counselors, as we noted. Several counselors (and one supervisor) complained that the director had "favorites" to whom he gave special attention, such as going out to lunch with them.[3] And both administrators were criticized for making too much money compared with counselors' salaries.

However, the most nagging problems that counselors encountered in their work were said to be due to the "contract situation" and to the board's power combined with its lack of knowledge of and genuine concern for the agency and its clientele. The administrators were bystanders. Counselor B, when asked if the administration was sympathetic to the counselors' problems, replied that "because of the contract situation, they can't always be sympathetic." He added that "they are doing all they can to solve the problems, but the numbers of clients required by the contracts cause many problems and pressures." When asked what changes he would make if he were director of the agency, Counselor D mentioned more training and more remedial programs for clients—and added that he "would try to raise more private money, so as not to depend on government money. They [government contracts] limit you." When asked the same question, Counselor G said: "I'd look for people . . . who could keep this place solvent. That way, you don't have to compromise or play politics in sustaining the agency. A large proportion of our money is from government grants. So that dictates that you play some politics, and make some compromises."

The counselors were also in agreement that the board reserved all genuine power for itself. When asked whether staff meetings were tightly controlled by the administrators, Counselor F said that "cut and dried" would be a better description: "Usually there's not that much to discuss. For example, when the Director calls a meeting after he's been to the Board meeting, he simply wants to let us know those things that went on: fund-raising statistics, the status of contracts, etc."

One or two meetings had been "very emotional," she said. She gave as an example the meeting where the board's decision to limit services to 16- to–19-year-old clients was announced. There had been "a lot of heavy going involving this directive from the Board," the counselor said. However, there was little the staff or the administrators could do about the decision, and overall the meeting was "kind of boring" because the counselors could only listen to the administrators "say why we couldn't expect certain things, given this change."

Counselor A, while criticizing the agency's "managerial procedures," acknowledged that the board was the real problem. He said that the director, as a type, was "a necessity these days" and added that "you have to have a certain type of Black who can get along with the establishment." One reason the board hired him, the counselor said, is that "they could work with him."

Counselor J, asked the same question, replied that "given the amount of power the Director has in this agency, I don't think there is much that could be done." "The Director has a function," he said, but added, "Mostly, the policies are dictated by the Board."

The picture that emerged was that of an administration that had little real control of events, perhaps because it was caught in the middle between two powerful forces: contract demands and the power of the board. Although the administrators negotiated the contracts and had access to the board, the evidence does not indicate that the counselors held them responsible for the problems that were mounting in the agency.

The counselors not only saw the board as having the power to make and enforce policy, they were also in open disagreement with the board over the substance of some policies. For example, Counselor J said that the board's decision to limit agency services to clients 16 to 19 years of age was "completely discriminatory" and was based on the assumption that the younger clients "need more help than anybody." In order for the agency to exist, he said, "we have to make a certain number of placements"; however, older clients "open the doors that allow the younger ones to get jobs." The board's new policy, he said, was like "getting some rope and hanging yourself, because the job market is not geared for the employment of 16 to 19 year olds."

For this same counselor, the agency's exclusive emphasis upon placement is also counterproductive:

All I'm doing now is saying, "Hey! You dropped out? Okay, fine! Let me give you a messenger job." How long is he going to last in a messenger job? What's he going to do after that? You're just recycling the same thing . . . . It will give him some financial help at home. But . . . unless you have schooling or . . . some kind of training program for them, it's useless.

When asked if involvement in union activities played any part in who got laid off after the addict program contract was not renewed, one counselor said he "really couldn't say, because one of the grievances of the staff was the fact that the personnel practices that we have are . . . backward and archaic . . . and it just gives administration total power in terms of everything." The effect of the personnel practices was that staff members "could be fired or laid off . . . without reason, at any time." The policy had been changed in this way by "the lawyers of the Board" about a year earlier.

Perhaps for these reasons, some counselors questioned the board's knowledge of agency affairs and the level of commitment board members have for the agency's clients and staff. Counselor J argued that it was difficult for the board "to say what's really best for clients" when the board members are "so out of touch with them." Counselor G was asked if the proposal to have staff representation on the board was important to the counselors. He replied: "Yeah, it's a big gripe with the staff . . . because they are not too convinced of the Board's commitment to the kids. So they [the staff] thought with their input they could convince the Board towards increased commitment to the kids."

For Counselor G, the biggest question about the board members' motivation and commitment was raised by the fact that "there are no poor people on the Board." For this reason, he thought that evaluation of the agency's work in terms of placements was desirable and important because only in this way could YEA be "held accountable to the community."

In brief, the attempt at unionization was a "message of discontent" to the administrators and an attempt to deal directly with the board as an equal or near-equal party. However, it was noted that it was the counselors' current work frustrations and insecurity that were focused on the board.

The problem of relations with the board was not a new one. There had been a general staff organization as far back as 1974. In the minutes of its first meeting on July 2 of that year, it was noted that the board of directors would meet in August for the purpose of "developing a rationale for the present structural framework of YEA." The minutes show that it was the "general consensus of the staff that we too must verbalize and formulate a philosophy from our particular perspective of daily interaction with our clients." This formulation of agency "philosophy" might "complement, augment, or even contradict the philosophy of the Board of Directors." Accordingly, the staff took the position that the board should be acquainted with their views "either through the Executive Director, *representation* [on the Board], or a position paper."

As we have noted, it appeared that the outlook of the counselors also became more bureaucratic in certain ways. That is, the changes were associated with personnel demands for some of the benefits of bureaucracy, including clearer standards of performance and evaluation (even though placement quotas were rejected), an end to arbitrary rule by the board, and a more rational salary structure, both among counselors and between counselors and administrators. These demands were expressed in staff meetings but were most emphatically expressed in the formation of the Staff Council (an internal organization of front-line personnel), in the unionization of staff, and in the proposal for staff representation on the board. It may seem odd to discuss unionization as manifesting a desire for greater bureaucratization of the agency. However, we must bear in mind what the counselors were seeking and view unionization as a means toward those ends.

Weber's work on bureaucracy can be seen as both a catalog of some of the benefits of bureaucracy and an exchange relationship between an organization and its personnel.[4] Bureaucracies are said to provide "increased guarantees against . . . arbitrary removal from office," a "mechanical fixing of the conditions of promotion" and salary levels, and a "secured money salary connected with the opportunity of a career that is not dependent upon mere accident and arbitrariness." In exchange for the predictability of conditions and rewards, and for rationality of rule, the bureaucrat commits himself to full-time loyal service: "Entrance into an office . . . is considered an acceptance of a specific obligation of faithful management in return for a secure existence."

Weber had in mind a secure and stable organization. However, when the organization itself becomes somewhat insecure and potentially unstable, as occurred at YEA, one strategy of the personnel appears to be a demand for greater bureaucratization. At YEA, these demands were addressed to the problem of insecurity but were also based on longstanding grievances that were held in abeyance as long as the agency was permitted to perform according to its "discretion" rather than detailed performance criteria, and as long as the labor market for clients and counselors was more favorable. But as agency and counselors were boxed in, the predictability and security of bureaucracy became more attractive to the counselors. In other words, new conditions (such as greater accountability, dependence, and insecurity) were associated with changes in the loyalties, task, and technology of the work and with new demands and strategies of a bureaucratic nature. These had to do with greater protection, predictability, and perquisites. Protection was desired against the exercise of arbitrary power by the patrimonially structured agency—especially but not exclusively arbitrary layoffs and firings—and involved unionization of the staff as well as proposals for staff representation on the board. Predictability was closely related to this but had as its essential aim the formation of rules and standards that would dispose of some of the uncertainty that surrounded performance evaluation. In uncertain conditions, the counselors seemed to want to know how they were doing (and possibly to be able to outdo others).

The concern for perquisites such as salaries involved both an alleged arbitrariness and a lack of predictability: Some "favored" counselors were paid more than others; counselors in general were paid far less than administrators; and there were no known standards for salary increases and promotions. In general, as security and discretion waned, attention was focused on the adequacy and fairness of compensation and other perquisites such as compensatory time and praise for work well done.

The unionization may have been of the shortest duration ever recorded—it lasted only a few days—but when counselors were asked why they thought the decision to unionize had been reached, they all referred to the problem of insecurity, among other reasons. One counselor replied: "I know what people were saying. They were saying that there were gross inequalities in salaries, favoritism . . . and also the fear of layoffs" because of the possible loss of the addict program contract. Another said that unionization was promoted by a "bunch of people trying to protect their own interests . . . job insecurity, for ex-

ample." When a third referred to a feeling of "paranoia," he meant that
"there's been a lot of talk about layoffs . . . and the first thing you do
is run for some type of security."

We must note, however, that the unionization involved more than
insecurity. The counselors have had a long-standing conflict with the
board over the virtually exclusive emphasis on placement. For the most
part, this took the form of "griping" as long as placements could be
made. As the city's job market deteriorated and the demand for unskilled and uneducated labor declined progressively, the counselors experienced more and more difficulty in accomplishing the placement
mission. Simultaneously, new contracts emphasized placement quotas,
and these were monitored by more rigorous procedures. Under these
conditions, the board reaffirmed the placement aspect of the agency's
mission but made it more difficult to attain by lowering the age limit
on the clients the agency would serve. The counselors apparently came
to feel that the board was too far removed from the work of the agency
(and too little interested in it) to understand the problems that ensued
from their policy decisions. The administration was too weak and ineffective in presenting the reality the counselors had to deal with to the
board. Perhaps with more emotion than reason, the union was seen by
some as a means of affording them more power in dealing with the
board on this issue—so as to make the agency more "bureaucratic" in
certain ways.

THE HAMMER AND THE TONG IN THE HANDS OF ADMINISTRATORS

It was no pleasure to observe the administrators' response to the
agency's problems and their attempts to explain them. When the executive staff met on May 16, the director had announced the loss of the
addict program contract, as we noted earlier. Following that announce-
ment the administrators and supervisors attempted to explain why the
staff had resorted to unionization. Their explanations were for the most
part quite varied. The counseling supervisor said that the blame should
fall on the counselors themselves because they did not "come to the
Executive Committee for resolutions to their problems and to air their
grievances." The OJT supervisor felt that the executive staff had fo-
mented discontent by "airing our grievances" against each other "in
front of everyone." The director's administrative assistant also blamed
the executive staff for failure to "project a stronger image" than the union
did in "solving staff problems." She also observed that there were some
"flaws in personnel practices" and gave as an example the fact that "the
conditions under which counselor probation is extended are not spelled
out" in detail. The director had other explanations. The need for "bet-

ter functioning" of the executive staff was demonstrated, he said, as was the need for "consistent direction" by administrators and supervisors: "Go to six different people and you get six different answers." In addition, counselors had been prevented or discouraged from seeing him; his open-door policy had not been effective for that reason. The director also noted that "we do not fire people quickly enough," which caused "subjectivity later on."

However, two explanations for the unionization were repeatedly mentioned. One was that the staff merely needed more information about the workings of and the constraints on the agency. The other explanation frequently advanced was that the problem was caused by a few malcontents on the staff.

The OJT supervisor said that "we should clearly inform the staff about contract job lines and the possibility that they will be terminated if the contract is cut," and that "it should be emphasized to the staff that if we do not spend all our employer-subsidy monies, the remainder . . . cannot be applied to salaries." The job development supervisor said that "we should explain the workings of the agency" to staff members. The addict program supervisor proposed a similar explanation in saying that the staff needed to "receive reports from the Director, just as the Board receives reports." The associate director added that "copies of the contracts, minus the budget, should be put in the library for the staff to read."

Several members of the executive staff also blamed the problem on a few "malcontents." The administrative assistant said that "it was one or two people who started the unionization movement." The job development supervisor agreed that one or two people who feared the loss of their jobs "started the movement, on the assumption that the union could save their jobs," and asked what "management techniques would be used in working with the few malcontents." The addict program supervisor noted that when the staff "realized that the people who began the movement were in it for personal reasons," most of them "pulled out."

Partly because the only agreement among the executive staff members was on the two explanations involving the staff's need for more information and on a few malcontents as the real problem, the administrators and supervisors were not greatly troubled by the attempt at unionization. The associate director said that "YEA is a great agency" and that "we should not over-react to the situation." The counseling supervisor was impatient with the discussion because "we have an agency to run and work that is not being done." The job development supervisor said that while communication in the agency could be better, "YEA is no better and no worse than any other organization" and that the executive staff "should not over-react." The addict program supervisor observed that "at this time, the staff is mixed up"; however, this was said to require only that "we step in and . . . guide them."

There were some superficial agreements between the complaints of the counselors and the explanations of the executive staff. For example, the fear of layoffs appeared to have been a factor in development of the union movement; however, it was not confined to "a few malcontents." Second, the personnel practices manual, mentioned by the administrative assistant, was also the object of complaint by Counselor J; however, his complaint was directed more toward what the manual *specified* in terms of power relations than to what it did *not* specify.

However, the executive staff members seemed to be unaware of some of the other major problems mentioned by counselors, including:

1. The "total power" of the board and administration
2. The administrators' isolation from the day-to-day work and their alleged high-handedness
3. The frustrations of the work, and pressures to produce placements under increasingly difficult conditions
4. Salary inequities, especially the gap between counselors' and executive staff salaries.

Closer analysis of the executive staff's explanations also shows that each "explanation" is actually an indictment of some other member(s) of the executive staff. When the director talked about "inconsistent direction" he was referring to the inconsistency of *the others*. And it was the others who prevented staff from seeing him. When the job development supervisor talked about malcontents, she was criticizing those other supervisors and the administrators who permitted the malcontents to remain on staff. When the OJT supervisor said that there was too much open disagreement among executive staff, she meant that the others talked about her in front of the counselors.

The executive staff continued to attack one another at a subsequent meeting, without ever discussing the basic complaints of the counselors. The director had already crushed the union by May 17, by reporting that the board would close down the agency rather than accept a union. Loss of the addict program contract came at just the right time to dramatize this threat. If layoffs were necessary, the agency could at least use them as an opportunity to "get rid of dead wood" (as the associate director described it)—including some of those active in the union.

The topic of the May 19 meeting of the executive staff was "What we want from the director." Minutes of the meeting are quite detailed and the statements by participants appear to be unusually candid. It appeared that the magnitude of the agency's recent problems brought to a head some long-standing complaints. At the meeting the supervisors criticized each other, they criticized the director for administrative deficiencies, and, along with the associate director, they criticized the director for certain personal failings.

Criticism of other supervisors took up the least time. The addict program supervisor said that other supervisors and the administrators should "stay in their own area" and not interfere with each other's performance of duty. The counseling supervisor observed that two other supervisors were frequently in the back of the office and "many times do not see their staff leaving early."

The director was subjected to frequent criticism for failures in administration. One supervisor said that "detailed job descriptions for Executive Staff" were needed because no one knew the duties and responsibilities clearly, and that "tighter leadership" was needed. Another said that a "constant state of crisis" was characteristic of YEA's administration. A third complained that members of the staff committee met with the director only, rather than with the executive staff as a whole. She added that "staff meetings should not interfere with the work day" and that enforcement of rules was lax, especially those related to working hours. Another charged that "we make big plans, but never follow through."

The director was criticized, in addition, for having "black moods." One supervisor said that she wanted an "even climate" in the agency, one "free from worrying about the moods of the administration." She also said that the director should not make "conflicting promises," and that his "promises should be kept." The OJT supervisor complained about the director's "lack of consideration and unintentional disrespect" for her and added the charge that he showed favoritism toward some staff members such as the one teacher who continued "to do what he wants while other staff members are reprimanded." The fiscal administrator also referred to the problem of the director's moods: "The swing of moods in the office that affect all of us should be ended." The associate director may have been the most blunt of all. The director, he said, was "part of the problem" the agency faced. There was a problem in "how he says things." Moreover, he failed to "show confidence in each of us here" and made "unrealistic demands." Finally, he was guilty of "snubbing people who are trying to relate something to him."

The director replied in detail to the charges. As far as favoritism was concerned, he said that the teacher who had not conformed to the agency's dress policy would be "terminated as of 30 July 1976 unless he conforms" and that he would send a memo to the teacher stating this. He had often been accused of favoritism with regard to one counselor, the director observed, but he asserted that he had never interfered with that counselor's "tenure." He asked the counseling supervisor if he had ever interfered with her supervision, and she replied he had not. The director then added that the evaluation of counselors was "in the hands of the supervisors."

As for his moods, the director said that he was "impatient with people who ramble on or are repetitious." This was, in part, the source of his moods. In addition, he said he was "plagued with issues that have already been resolved," so that no further discussion should be required. However, he pledged to do what he could to control his "black moods" since a "less personal climate in the agency is called for."

As for enforcement of rules, he stated, existing ones should be enforced "until the new Personnel Practices is written and approved by the Board." He added that "the enforcement of staff hours lies with each individual supervisor."

He then asked the associate director what he meant by "unrealistic demands." The associate director replied that "it sounded good in the context of what I was thinking." That reply seemed to trigger the director's anger. The associate director's office, he said, "takes too long to pull together statistics," and the day before his administrative assistant "had to re-do the report to the Mayor's office" because it was "poorly done." The director then warned that he did not want lies and that staff members should be "careful not to be caught in a lie."

In addition, he charged that the agency's paperwork was not done on time and that "the staff has time to fool around." To the associate director he said, "I will require you to get out of your office more and walk the halls." Currently, he said, the associate director was "making too many assumptions," and an "unfair burden" was being shifted to the supervisor of counseling.

To emphasize the authority structure of the agency, the director pointed out that "one person runs the agency here—and I am the one who makes the decisions to be carried out." This responsibility might be shared with the executive staff, and they were free to express disagreements, but "the final decision is mine." Nor would the staff run YEA, he said: "The Board of Directors run YEA" and only they "designate an Executive Director to follow Board policy." The board had threatened to "close the agency rather than unionize," he said; however, the administration should "maintain an atmosphere of good will in dealing with the staff."

We might assume that the meeting was even more acrimonious than the record shows.[5] The members of the executive staff ganged up on the director for his moods, his snubs, his favoritism, and so on—but did not, in the process, neglect each other for laxness, for not following through on agreed-upon decisions, and for interference in each other's areas of responsibility. The director acknowledged his alleged faults but turned the situation around to show that the others were really at fault for rambling on, being repetitious, lying, and so on. The other executive staff members were put in their place. They were without any formal authority and shared in the decision-making only insofar as the director allowed them to. The board possessed ultimate authority, and it delegated that authority only to the executive director. In this respect the supervisors and the associate director were in the same position as the counselors.

The unionization and loss of the addict program contract were major events in YEA. The shock waves were felt for some time afterward. The agency personnel appeared to be merely walking through their duties and in low spirits. The director seemed to spend more time than usual alone in his office. He was, in the words of the associate director, "like a general who has lost his country, but is still in his little room—giving orders just like nothing happened." Not one general staff meeting was held in the four or five weeks that elapsed between the time the staff was notified of the contract loss and the time the field work was completed.

Counselor J was asked how he would describe the morale of the counselors who were remaining after the layoffs. He replied: "Morale is at a low. I think when you walk around, you can't help seeing it. It's staring you in the face." He mentioned the "empty offices" and the "flashbacks, of people just laughing, or just people . . . " What about the Staff Council? he was asked. What is it doing? He said, "People have no gripes now. They are just worried about keeping their jobs. Everything else is secondary." For Counselor J, the layoffs made the Staff Council and the union useless: "I mean the actual thing the union was started for *occurred*. And nothing could be done to stop it. Nothing could be done now." The counselors were extremely insecure, he said. They felt that "if things could happen that quickly" in the addict program layoffs, then "the same thing could happen again. They're on their toes."

If the council were active, we asked, would staff contact with the board still be a main issue? How important was that? He replied: "I think at this point people just don't care . . . . The only issue people have is just trying to keep the job they have . . . and not making waves."

Counselor G characterized the staff at this stage as showing "more confusion than anything." But he also noted, "A lot of people now are worried about further cuts . . . . They are not putting forth as much effort."

The bureaucratic mode of production imposed on YEA was in part responsible for the events reported here, such as weeding out marginal clients for the sake of productivity. However, this change also depended upon the existence of a great deal of uncertainty involving both the continued existence of the agency and the daily work of the counselors. The resulting insecurity, in turn, appeared to trigger a latent conflict between counselors and the board, and to lead the counselors to seek greater security in bureaucratic rules regarding tenure and compensation. Thus, not only did the work itself become more bureaucratic, but the outlook of the workers changed, veering from a relatively altruistic absorption in the work itself to a preoccupation with bureaucratic solutions to certain important work problems. Without considering the purposes of the work, this change, by itself, might be of limited interest. However, there is reason to believe that the effect of this transformation was to change what was a rather effective system (based on counselor altruism and organizational discretion) into a less-effective system for dealing with the problem of unemployment in a young, marginally qualified population.

NOTES

1. The administrative assistant later withdrew in recognition of her conflict of interest—but not before effectively "spying" for the director.

2. This might be interpreted as some gain by staff, in that at least they would know about the openings. This would be a gain, however, only if they did not know about them in the past. What little evidence is available on this suggests that in general staff members were not officially and consistently informed about openings, but that unofficially there was knowledge of them. Thus, the inclination is to see little change here in reality, especially since the supervisors could make particular choices. However, the formal acknowledgment of the staff's "right" in this respect might be construed as a gain.

3. The director was criticized for being isolated and not being involved with the staff—and at the same time, he was criticized for liking certain staff members, that is, having "favorites." Apparently, the counselors and supervisors wanted him to like them all equally—with each one preferring that he like him or her a little more than the others.

4. Max Weber, "Bureaucracy," in *From Max Weber: Essays in Sociology*, ed. Hans Gerth and C. Wright Mills (New York: Oxford University Press, 1946). See pp. 203, 208, and 199.

5. This is supported by a comment made by the associate director in one of our conversations. The administrative assistant, he said, was "good at writing up the meetings, but even she [did] not get in the full flavor" of the meetings.

9

Regrouping and Moving Forward

The counselors' malaise did not last indefinitely. By late 1978, when YEA was visited again, the agency had resumed its expansion. The staff had increased in size to 56 people, with projections of up to 70 employees within two years. More space was needed. Since none was available in the building, the existing space was being partitioned in a way that would yield more offices. The budget was around $1.5 million, and the assistant director anticipated a budget of $2 million soon, "if we hustle." The advocacy role of the agency was being further developed. A nationally distributed *You and Youth* newsletter was being planned, to be written for industrial and commercial subscribers. The purpose of the newsletter was to report on youth employment programs around the country, informing employers about available programs and "demolishing myths" about youthful workers, particularly those with correctional backgrounds. The newsletter would employ 25 part-time "stringers" in major cities of the country to write about their local programs and related events. It was emphasized, however, that the newsletter would supplement rather than replace the current activities, such as job placement. The current activities also included a new cycle of drafting trainees. Other new developments included, for the first time, stipends for clients in the remedial-education program, and something called "the work world project," in which a handbook for small, neighborhood agencies engaged in job placement was being prepared. "It's the first time we've been able to sell YEA's technology in this way," the assistant director reported with obvious enthusiasm and pride.

There was little personnel turnover. Except for Counselor D and Counselor H, all were still there. The executive director was also still at his post. He had considered a position with a foundation but was talked out of it by the chairman. "We have an agreement," the director said. "He told me to stay with YEA for now, then 'we will consider your career.' " Further growth was planned and consolidation of the new projects required his continued leadership for the time being. The over-all outlook was one of optimism, with no recognition that the agency and the work of its counselors had been transformed. It seems fitting to conceptualize the change more clearly here, and to relate this to the contract form before offering a few concluding remarks.

We recall that the percentage of clients who did not return to YEA after the initial interview increased substantially in the 1974–76 period, compared with an earlier three-year period. This change coincided with the agency's involvement in the first of its large contracts in which pro-gram accountability was spelled out in considerable detail. The per-centage of "one-interview clients" was seen as an indicator that some clients were "weeded out." This was accomplished by leaving it up to the client to "keep in touch" with the counselor, as opposed to earlier agency practice. Interviews with counselors suggested that this became a new "test" of the client's "motivation." In the earlier period counsel-ors had assumed responsibility for maintaining contact with clients and encouraging them with job openings. This change in agency practice was associated with changes in the job market for both clients and counselors and with the agency's increased dependence on contracts with other organizations as sources of funds.

In general it appeared that the counselors' criterion of motivation ("keeping in touch") weeded out the clients who needed help the most: the youngest, the least educated, and the least experienced. These clients were more difficult to place on jobs and were sacrificed by the agency under the increasing pressure to meet placement and retention quotas. The change appears to be associated with a new type of contract that demanded greater accountability. The new contracts did not com-pletely eliminate the counselors' efforts to place individual clients by "reaching out" for them, but apparently the effort was more selective and was most focused upon clients sufficiently "motivated" to keep in touch with the counselor. The avowed purpose of the funded pro-grams (and the agency itself), on the other hand, was to assist the *least qualified* to gain employment. This goal appeared to have been achieved under the older, more traditional "best-effort contracts." Under these contracts "hard-to-place clients" were encouraged to return for service. The newer performance contracts thus appear to have resulted in the weeding out of just those clients the agency and the contract were de-signed to serve.

Rationalized accountability also had the tendency of orienting the or-ganization's activity to generating those categories of statistics that pro-vided for additional funding. The agency and counselors, often with-out knowing it, abandoned their original mission in order to generate accountability statistics so as to ensure the survival of the organization.

Centrally for YEA, the rationalization of standards in the performance contracts resulted in a sacrifice in its original mission, placement of hard-core unemployed, in order to gain and maintain contracts. The new contracts resulted in the agency and its counselors' placing *less* demand upon themselves as defined by the intensity of service to clients, and a change in the characteristics of clients, serving the most easily and "objectively" served while cooling and weeding out the others. A change in the target population was the ultimate outcome. The hard-core problem client became increasingly isolated from services because serving him or her produced poor or unrewarding statistics.

This process was facilitated by bureaucratic categorizations and standards. To a government bureaucracy, the problem was a categorical one: drug addicts, delinquents, and so on. All were equally "deserving." Thus it made little difference if some were weeded out as long as those who were serviced met the formal criteria for service and were satisfactorily processed. This increased productivity but conflicted with the counselors' altruistic tendency to help the most needy among the category and conflicted also with the agency's traditional mission. Here, the altruistic orientation was outweighed by the bureaucratic one.

We can better analyze the effects of this process on the work of the counselors if we make a distinction between "bureaucratic" and "altruistic" work, which is done in Table 9.1. (The latter may not be the best term for non-bureaucratic work, but perhaps the characteristics of the two will help explain why it is used here.) The advantage of the typology is that it shows more specifically how altruistic work can become bureaucratized. The reader familiar with organizational theory will note that for the most part this classification involves merely an attempt to more narrowly define, dichotomize, and categorize standard concepts such as technology, nature of material, structural relations, repetitive operations, labor intensity, mode of production, and unit of production.

The task of bureaucratic organizations and their personnel is *production*, carried out in accordance with certain norms involving the "objective discharge of business . . . according to *calculable rules* and without regard for persons" and emphasizing "precision, steadiness, and, above all, the speed of operations."[1] With this goes an orientation toward "cases" as units of production and counting cases as a means of assessing production. The task of such organizations and certain personnel also usually includes the creation and maintenance of demand, as opposed to merely meeting demand. The loyalty of personnel is to their superiors and ultimately to the organization.[2]

Altruistic organizations and their personnel, on the other hand, have as their principal task the modification or "repair" of material (clients). The loyalty of the personnel is divided between the clientele and the organization, with a tendency toward stronger loyalty to clients. The

Table 9.1
Typology of Bureaucratic and Altruistic Work

Category	"Bureaucratic"	"Altruistic"
ALLEGIANCE	Organization	Material (client)
TASK	Production	Modification or "repair"
ETHIC	Exploiting	Helping
RELATIONS	Instrumental	Expressive
OPERATIONS	Standardized-repetitive	Diagnostic-reflective
STANDARDS	Absolute	Relative
CONTROLS	Monitoring	Responsibility
STRUCTURE	Interdependent units	Autonomous units
OBJECT ORIENTATION	(1) "Bias" towards work-able material (2) "Concern" over out-come patterns	(1) "Bias" towards prob-lem material/clients (2) "Concern" over indi-vidual outcomes
INTELLECTUAL ORIENTATION	Abstract-categorical; rule formulation	Concrete-particular; problem solving
PRINCIPAL RESOURCES	Machines and mechanistic systems	Language and meanings
WORKER/PRODUCT RATIO	Low	High
WORKER UNIT OF PRODUCTION	Component or undiffer-entiated mass	Discrete whole
RHYTHM OF PRODUCTION	Steady	Sporadic

quality of task performance is more highly regarded than is quantity. The organization is oriented toward meeting the demand for service; specialized personnel may attempt to assess demand or sell the services, but do not attempt to create or maintain demand since demand is based on the existence of misfortune.

The changes in work performance at YEA were first and foremost in the areas of task and loyalty, shifting from "repair" to production and from client loyalty to organizational loyalty. These shifts were evident in the technology. *Operations* became more standardized in that there were fewer diagnostic categories: Clients were either job ready or not.

And diagnosis was increasingly supplanted by standardized manipulation ("persuasion") as counselors tried to get clients to accept the available jobs. The *structure* of the organization was increasingly composed of independent units, such as the job preparation workshop and the post-placement counselors, rather than more autonomous ones. Changes in *object orientation* were evident in the practice of weeding out clients who were not going to be easily placed. *Standards* tended to become more absolute: Clients had to keep in touch with the counselors; and for the organization, placement and retention rates and unit costs replaced those more relative to labor market conditions and the clientele, for example. And *controls* on the agency increasingly took the form of monitoring—for example, placement performance and unit costs—although direct controls on the workers did not change.

It has been (and is) difficult to avoid viewing these changes as negative ones, and in certain ways they undoubtedly were. At the same time, this kind of judgment is not altogether useful. Old buildings are torn down and replaced because, with new buildings springing up all around, the space cannot be rented. For the same kind of reasons, YEA probably had to change if it wanted to maintain its services and, almost certainly, if it wanted to expand and "modernize." Large-scale governmental involvement in manpower services may have altered the environment of YEA in irreversible ways. But to refrain from judgment is not to abandon analysis.

Vidich and Bensman wrote that in studying Springdale their "central concern was with the processes by which the small town (and indirectly all segments of American society) are continuously and increasingly drawn into the central machinery, processes and dynamics of the total society."[3] Springdale was controlled far more by "centralization, bureaucratization and dominance by large-scale organizations" than its residents knew. We could say the same thing about YEA and similar organizations, with contractual relationships and financial dependence providing the connection between small philanthropic organizations and large government bureaucracies. But more than exposure of the "bureaucratic connection" is involved. Bureaucracy, left to its own devices, both intensifies and becomes the instrument of a supreme indifference.

MASTERS AND SLAVES

Bureaucratic organizations define their work (and gauge their success) predominantly in terms of rationality. Goals of a substantive nature matter less than rationalization of the work itself and the relationship of officials. The smooth, predictable, orderly transaction of work is of the greatest significance. Strategies based on dependence, the elimination of personal factors and feelings ("passion"), and rational accountability—visible in the streams of reports flowing upward—are purely instrumental.

Max Weber was the first sociologist to conceptualize and analyze the phenomenon of bureaucracy and to explain the spread of bureaucracy in modern societies on the basis of its "technical superiority" to all other forms of organization, given the conditions and demands created by democracy, capitalism, modern technology, and the spirit of rationality characteristic of modern societies. "The modern state is absolutely dependent upon a bureaucratic basis," he observed, especially when it is large and "becomes a great power state." However, bureaucracies are also essential for the "organized, collective, inter-local and thus bureaucratic provision for the most varied of wants" for the populace, and for carrying out the "manifold tasks" of social welfare programs that are in part "saddled upon the state by interest groups" and in part usurped by the state. Not only is the modern state bureaucratized, but "the very large modern capitalist enterprises are themselves unequaled models of strict bureaucratic organization." The "special virtue" of bureaucracy is its success in "eliminating from official business love, hatred, and all purely personal, irrational, and emotional elements which escape calculation."[4]

For Perrow, the significance of bureaucracy is that by virtue of its indispensability, size, and structure, it centralizes more and more power in the hands of individual "masters."[5] Here, we add that the employees of contracting agencies such as YEA are increasingly exposed to bureaucratic orientations and practices through contractual relationships and "affiliations" that impose bureaucratic masters upon them.

Another way of stating this is to say that the "masters" in modern welfare states include powerful government bureaucracies, and that their mastery is based in part on the kind of rational, impersonal thinking of which they were, in Weber's view, the progenitors. That is, the modern world, including industrial organizations, has been profoundly influenced by bureaucratic relationships and thought processes. Welfare institutions are increasingly coming under the sway of bureaucratic thinking, just as industrial organizations have done. The total effect of this, both quantitatively and qualitatively, makes the process a significant one. The masters, of course, become slaves also—slaves to higher masters, but also slaves to the bureaucratic apparatus they supposedly control.

In the American welfare state, based on the primacy of self-dependence, as expenditures and the number of programs increase there appears to be an increased emphasis on accountability. The outlook and the expertise of bureaucracies lie in the development of abstract standards as the basis of a rationalized system that will permit comparability and assessment of results. When decentralization is the order of the day—such as in the CETA program—and accountability is still required of the federal agencies, the possibilities for deviations and variations become too great to handle. Standards become even more important— standards for conceiving of goals and means, and for allocating funds as well as accounting for them. The bureaucratic mission of the federal agency becomes that of standardizing all that comes within its purview. Paradoxically, decentralization may result in greater centralization than ever. The mission of the bureaucracy in this sense conflicts with the missions of smaller units such as YEA, with the latter stressing uniqueness rather than standardization, discretion rather than accountability, and a monopoly on the problem rather than competition.

The board of directors of YEA were aware of this intrusion of bureaucracy. We observed the resistance they offered in seeking to carry out the agency's mission in a universe of standardization and accountability, and we saw that they were caught in a dilemma: how to keep the agency going when private funds were increasingly difficult to raise. But they were not aware of the extent of bureaucratic intrusion. Only accidentally did they discover how agency personnel deviated from the agency's mission in their attempt to meet contract quotas and standards. And board members have as yet no inkling of the fragmentation of the agency into separate programs based on different contracts. The intimacy and unity between administrators and counselors, and between counselors and clients, appear to have been weakened.

Counselors increasingly had to be evaluated and controlled in order to meet contract quotas. Although the administrators were not notably successful in this, their failure resulted in increased hostility and resentment as they pressed counselors to keep busy and to refrain from talking to one another. The meaning of the work was also affected by the necessity of eliminating clients in order to achieve objective measures of success according to contract specifications, and the clients became more a means to an end than they formerly had been. The counselors initiated new procedures to satisfy contract demands for placements by concentrating their work on certain clients and weeding out the others. The mission of the agency was altered de facto in the attempt to implement de jure definitions under new conditions. The "target population" of the contract programs, and the traditional clientele of the agency (the "hardest to place" clients), were served less effectively or hardly at all when the requirements for serving them became more specific and were coupled with penalties.

Some of the problems discussed here would seem to have rather straightforward, conventional solutions. For example, federal programs such as CETA could easily involve program operators and others in the planning stage, where goals and standards are set. This would go a long way toward making the goals and standards realistic, and would have the further advantage of making program operators partners in the effort. At present, the federal government is among the most backward of organizations in this respect.

However, since the federal government conducts much of its business by contract, even this change would be only minimally effective without some change in the form of contract used for social services. One reason for the poor results obtained from the ambitious programs of the sixties and seventies is that our "contract technology" has not kept up with the changing role of government.

The conventional contract is based on certain assumptions about the world and its actors. These include (1) that actors have sufficient knowledge of the matter to enter into a contract, (2) that events and acts are discrete and thus have no connection with other events and acts, (3) that the world is essentially static, at least for the life of the contract, (4) that suspicion toward the other party is an appropriate attitude, and, therefore, (5) that the interests of the parties should be reflected in the contract. On the basis of these assumptions, contracts can be and typically are in writing and they are specific, irrevocable and binding, closed, and adversarial in nature and form.

It is possible to make other assumptions on the basis of which another type of contract can be conceived. These assumptions would include (1) that actors (or parties) are sufficiently uncertain of the matter at hand to enter into a binding contract, (2) that acts and events interact with each other to produce outcomes, (3) that the world is constantly changing, even if in small, hardly discernible ways and granting that not all changes directly and immediately touch all, (4) that an attitude of trust toward the other party may be appropriate, and, therefore, (5) that the interests of society can and should be reflected in the contract.

A few comments on certain of these assumptions are necessary with respect to the assumption of "uncertainty." For example, it seems clear that the various theories about the motivation of workers—in the form of scientific management, human relations, hierarchical needs, self-actualization, participation, job enrichment, and so on—and the present-day marketing of numerous and diverse techniques (for example, "Seven Master Keys to Employee Handling—for the executive who wants every last ounce of sweat, loyalty, and dedication employees can give") suggest we have much to learn about the motivation of *all* workers, not just manpower "trainees." We simply don't know the long-range implications of our efforts, the career patterns we are shaping, and the ways in which we are contributing to mobility or, conversely, strengthening the class structure.

As for the interaction of events, it is clear that neither YEA's administrators nor its counselors planned to weed out marginal clients. Rather, this seems to have resulted from several forces working together: recession, job insecurity, and the imposition of narrowly defined performance standards, for example. In this situation, monitoring performance was not a "discrete" act. Finally, we must note that "suspicion" is often simply a self-fulfilling prophecy. There are undoubtedly times when it is appropriate—just as there are times when it is not. As long ago as the Hawthorne studies, we learned that trust and an accompanying sense of partnership paid off in productivity. The same point is made repeatedly in the latest articles on reindustrialization: The lack of trust deprives organizations of the willing and creative contributions of their workers. Not much has been done to implement this knowledge, but we have yet to even recognize its implications for contracts.

On the basis of these assumptions, then, a new form of "human-service contract" might be appropriate and feasible for at least some social services. A human-service contract should be more global than narrowly specific, evolutionary rather than irrevocable, open-ended instead of closed, and cooperative and reciprocal in its structure and implementation rather than adversarial. In principle, it should be "verbal" rather than written; this would not preclude exchanging written memorandums of understanding, but it would emphasize verbal assessments of performance including talking with staff and trainees rather than relying exclusively on statistical indicators.

In "global" contracts a range of desirable outcomes would be identified (and possibly weighted) as indicators of successful performance. In some cases these should be things we normally take for granted, such as attendance and attitudes toward working and supervision. There is no reason that progress in these areas should be ignored in the assessment of contract performance. They need not be weighted as heavily as other outcomes—for example, job placement—but their inclusion would give program operators a much-needed degree of flexibility as well as the possibility of achieving significant overall success through various combinations.

An "evolutionary" contract would have two dimensions: (1) During the life of the contract (if it has a definite term), targets or objectives are adjusted as conditions that affect the objectives change, and (2) progressively higher levels of achievement are sought (and rewarded), given favorable conditions and successful performance at lower levels of performance. "Irrevocable" contracts, by contrast, have the effect of inducing contractors to aim for easily attainable objectives, then locking them in to that level of performance. If conditions change for the worse, there is no out; if they change for the better, there is no incentive to aim higher.

An "open" contract refers to an ongoing contract with no end date specified—and no minimum term guaranteed (although a reasonable start-up period would need to be assured). The objectives would be to incorporate a longer-range view into the contractual relationship and to provide both a greater degree of financial security for program operators and a higher level of performance. The open contract would not preclude cancellation for failure to achieve progress as indicated by the more global criteria suggested or for failure to meet certain fundamental requirements such as the acceptance of clients, conducting a work-oriented program, and so forth. Termination of a contract would not be arbitrary, however, and might require a review of the case by outside experts before being put into effect.

A "cooperative-reciprocal" contract would involve an assumption of good faith in which both parties are avowedly and formally working toward the same goal, rather than being a punitive contract. It is not a one-way contract. Federal contracts at present have a way of being both these things. What is required, instead, is an advisory, consultative, mutual-assistance relationship. Perhaps there is no practical way this feature can be "written into" the contract. It may be that by implementing an evolutionary-open-global contract a "cooperative" one would result, especially if it were more "verbal" than written. The prospect of such a contract's being used in the near future is negligible, of course; its purpose here is analytical and illustrative. The construction of a model contract focuses attention on the features of existing contracts that contributed to the transformation of YEA and diminished its success in dealing with a specific clientele.

Ultimately, the success of YEA would probably be judged by most outsiders according to how effectively it sorts out those who want to work from those who do not. This carries us beyond bureaucratic standards. Even the standards to which YEA was held accountable required placement of only a certain calculated percentage of enrollees. There were not enough suitable jobs for all those physically available for work, and none for those not adjudged to be "motivated" to work.

The counselors appeared to reflect this view, whether they blamed the clients or weeded them out. Earlier in the agency's history, when jobs were available, the tendency was to think of the work as "job-matching," or putting the right client on the right job. This assumed and depended upon the availability of unskilled jobs of different kinds. More recently, the work has come to be seen as involving sorting out the clients into those who are ready for work (the "deserving") and those who are not (the "undeserving"). However, the losers withdraw from the competition (at least temporarily) rather than strive harder as they are supposed to do.

As for the counselors themselves, one could not help but be convinced of the presence of a special motivational ingredient in their work. Here, this has been discussed under the general heading of altruism.

Altruism did not always result in "good work," and not all counselors appeared to be equal in this respect. Some counselors may "hustle" altruism and exploit clients. Some counselors may exploit the financial opportunities inherent in a situation where money is "available for the taking." But for most counselors the altruistic ingredient produced "concerned" work, where the outcome mattered.

Titmuss observed that the incidence of altruism is dependent upon the existence of social institutions to permit the expression of altruism.[6] Giving blood, for example, is facilitated by the existence of blood banks and "blood drives." Similarly, assistance to disaster victims is undoubtedly increased by the existence of social organizations such as the Red Cross. But there is a distinction to be made between sporadic and sustained altruism, or between avocational and vocational altruism. Philanthropic organizations may facilitate the incidence of sporadic altruism (blood donations, canned goods, and clothing to disaster areas). But the staffing of organizations of this type also provides an opportunity for the expression of stronger-than-average altruistic impulses, at least in a relatively small part of the population, in the form of a career. The organizations do increase the incidence of altruism, as Titmuss observes. But the impulse, the altruistic "calling," seems to exist independent of the organizations.

Perhaps the broadest implication of the problem of altruism is that it may depend upon or be called into being by misfortune and inequality. The more societies eliminate or ameliorate misfortune, the less need there is for altruism and, presumably, the less altruistic behavior there will be. (This is quite contrary to Titmuss' position.) Good fortune (or better fortune) becomes more a matter of right, and altruism becomes an occupation—a calling in the service of social programs. In all likelihood, however, bureaucracies are created to carry out new missions. The trap in this is that, as Weber observed, the "special virtue" of the instrument selected is that it "dehumanizes" that which comes within its reach by "eliminating from official business love, hatred, and all purely personal, irrational, and emotional elements." Whether this contradiction can be resolved by altruism is a major question and one that we cannot answer here. Gerth and Mills observe that Weber regarded charismatic figures as "revolutionary forces" both in the past and in the present because charisma as a basis of legitimation of authority is "opposed to all institutional routines," either traditional ones or those based upon "rational management." Altruism may also be such a revolutionary and anti-bureaucratic force.[7] While it may be less revolutionary than charisma, it may at the same time be more attainable. Under present circumstances, bureaucratic organizations appear to distort, deflect, and constrain altruism. What emerges from the interaction between organizations and the altruistic impulse is what might be called, at best, a "lesser altruism." There is some irony in this fact, inasmuch as the organizations may themselves represent an altruistic endeavor.

NOTES

1. Max Weber, "Bureaucracy," in *From Max Weber: Essays in Sociology* eds. Hans Gerth and C. Wright Mills (New York: Oxford University Press, 1946).

2. Ibid., p. 199.

3. Arthur J. Vidich and Joseph Bensman, *Small Town in Mass Society* (Princeton, N.J.: Princeton University Press, 1968).

4. Max Weber, "Bureaucracy," pp. 211–16.

5. Charles Perrow, *Complex Organizations: A Critical Essay* (Glenview, Ill.: Scott, Foresman and Co., 1972). See pp. 197–203.

6. Richard M. Titmuss, *The Gift Relationship: From Human Blood to Social Policy* (New York: Vintage Books, 1972).

7. Hans Gerth and C. Wright Mills (eds.), *From Max Weber: Essays in Sociology* (New York: Oxford University Press, 1946). See p. 52 in their introduction.

Appendix A

YEA Organizational Chart, 1976

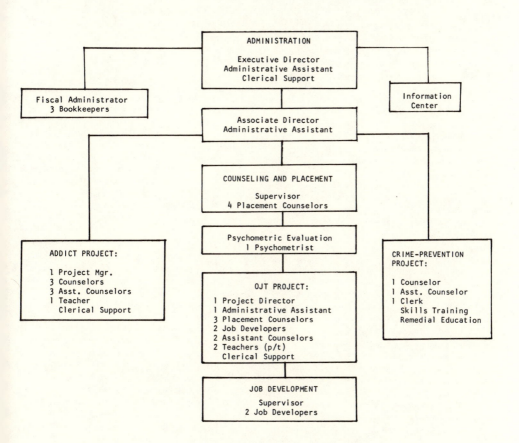

Appendix B
Client Flow Chart

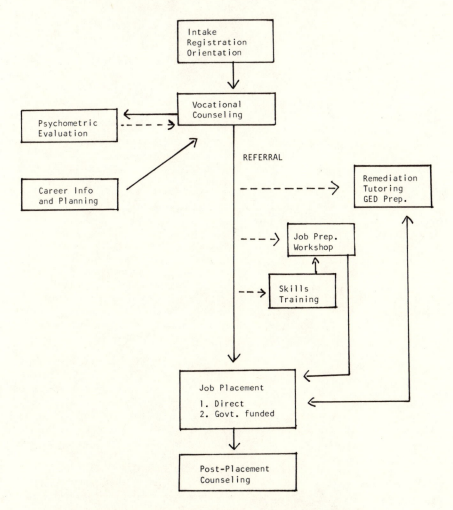

NOTE: Solid lines represent standard programming; broken lines represent optional programming.

Appendix C

Summary of YEA Statistical Reports

1. Internal Monthly Report

   A. Broken down by male, female
   B. Broken down by racial code
   C. Gives the following information
      New registrations
      Re-entry
      Client population age groups
         16-19
         20 and over
   D. Number of interviews
      Number of referrals
      Total number of placements
      F/T, P/T, Temporary, OJT
      Skills training
      Other training
      Number of clients tested
      Drug background
      Correctional background
      Past work experience
      Public assistance
      High school graduate

2. Internal Monthly Report Cover Sheets

   A. Broken down by contract vs. non-contract
   B. Gives monthly figures; cumulative-to-date figures; monthly
      figures for last year at the same time, and cumulative-to-
      date figures for last year
   C. Gives the following information
      Client populations
         New registrations
         Re-entry
      Fiscal year-to-date information
         16-19-year-olds
         Drug background

Correctional background
Past work experience
Public assistance
High school graduate
Total number of interviews
Job referrals
Total placements
F/T, P/t, Temporary, OJT
Skills training
Other training
Number of clients tested

Prepared in June 1976 by Associate Director's Administrative Assistant.

3. Monthly Remedial Education Report

Gives the following information
Broken down by age group and racial code
   Total number of clients in orientation
   Total number of new students
Broken down by age group and tupe of remedial
education given to client
   Total number of individuals seen during the month
   Number of clients completed course
   Number of clients left course
   Number of clients still attending
Number of GED received during month
Total number of sessions held during month
All figures cumulative to date.

4. Monthly "Youth Program" and "Ex-Addict Program" Reports

Intake forms-number of individuals accepted by YEA
Enrollment forms-number of individuals YEA will try to place
Termination forms-number of jobs actually gotten for those
 clients who were enrolled
30 consecutive workday follow-up forms
90-day follow-up forms
Monthly report cover sheet is cumulative to date.

5. Monthly "Crime-Prevention Program" Report

Voucher forms indicate number of individuals placed during month
Also indicates number of days clients already placed on jobs
have worked
Monies vouchered for per month and on a cumulative basis
Number of clients placed from different referral units of
contractor

6. Weekly counselor placement and referral sheets

Date of referral
Name of client referred
Referral agency
Date of referral
Date of hire

Reason for not hiring client
Cover sheet summarized all counselors' activities for the week

7. Internal Operations

Special statistical historical reports
Reports to the board of directors on all agency activities
Analyzing data from monthly reports
Submitting projections for the completion of contracts
Submitting proposals for possible new contracts based on
past performance

Appendix D

Example of a Christmas Fund-Raising Letter

This is the time of year when I write to my friends and seek to enlist their support for Youth Employment Agency. I am going to follow my usual pattern—with a long letter—because I am encouraged that my friends do read it and, thereby, do get an understanding of what YEA is all about.

This past year has been a most difficult one for the youngsters we serve and a challenging one for the agency. It is no cliché to call these youngsters for whom we get jobs "disadvantaged" for they truly are—by their poor educational backgrounds, their lack of skills, and their serious social disabilities. In addition, the job market, as you know, has tightened this year with devastating effects on the young who are at the bottom of the economic ladder.

Because it is a private, non-profit agency, YEA has been able to respond with flexibility to these conditions. For example, beyond its job placement and counseling services, YEA has undertaken a new pre-job skills program to strengthen basic 3-R capabilities which are nearly always lacking in our youngsters; further, it has also pursued job openings more vigorously than ever before in its history. At the end of the fiscal year, October 31, 1971, 2,218 jobs were secured for a record number of 2,720 youngsters counseled. Compared to last year's figures, which are indicated in the enclosed material, the performance for 1971 is remarkable.

To illustrate how YEA works with a typical youngster, I would like to tell you briefly about a young man (Marvin) who first came to the agency in the fall of 1968 when he was sixteen, following a term at the __Training School for Boys. He had been sent to this state training school because of his long record of school truancy, breaking and entering, and auto theft.

When he first came to us, Marvin made a decision to return to school and work part-time. YEA successfully placed him in a job. He dropped out of school, however, before completing ninth grade. Returning to YEA for full-time work, we placed him in several jobs. Because of his lack of skills and education, Marvin could qualify for only the most menial entry-level jobs. As you would expect, he found it difficult to make a satisfactory adjustment to the world of work. In the fall of 1969, Marvin was placed by YEA in a clerical training program in a bank where he also received remedial instruction in preparation for a high school equivalency diploma. By this time, Marvin was married and his wife was expecting a child. After a few months in the program, he was discharged for excessive lateness and absence. Again, he came back to YEA and the pattern of drifting in and out of entry-level jobs persisted.

During this entire period, a great many counseling sessions were held with Marvin. Because of his instability and immaturity, extra-ordinary amounts of time, as well as patience, were required from our counselors. Gradually, Marvin responded and began to gain an awareness of himself and his previous mistakes. In the summer of 1971, we were convinced he was ready to enter another clerical training program, this time with one of the leading textile corporations in the city. YEA has recently had a letter from the head of the company's personnel department indicating his gratitude for YEA's selection of applicants for the program and his satisfaction with the performance of the group. Marvin ranked high in that group.

This story of Marvin exemplifies the basic purpose of YEA. First, of course, is the commitment to help the youngster stand on his own feet and develop a mature attitude toward himself through a positive work experience. Marvin required a long time to reach this point—which is not unusual considering his age and his background. What is unusual and makes YEA unique is the continuing availability of the agency's services during this development process. The stages of Marvin's progress are typical of other youngsters and demonstrate so well how YEA meets the specific needs of these boys and girls.

I want to add that YEA also has a high sense of responsibility to the employer. We are deeply indebted to the companies which are willing to risk hiring young people who appear to be so hopelessly disadvantaged. The matching of the youngster to the job is carefully considered. The personnel manager of one firm wrote to us: "Your personal insight with the trainees has been invaluable . . . . The company has found an agency it can work with in complete confidence." This statement indicates the reaction we have had with many companies for whom we have performed this role.

The YEA staff and directors, of course, have a strong sense of obligation to the community at large. Through successful placements in jobs and training programs, these youths are being given a productive alternative to the life of the street. Drug addiction, crime, welfare dependence, all go hand in hand with the unemployment of these youngsters.

I again ask you to join me in a commitment to this exceptional program. Youth Employment Agency is dependent primarily on your support and assistance. We do receive funds from city, state and, sometimes, federal sources but the lifeblood of YEA is the support it receives from individuals, corporations and foundations. Please be as generous as your budget permits!

With best wishes for a pleasant holiday,

Sincerely,
W___ T___

P.S. Please make your check payable to Youth Employment Agency, and send it to me at this address. It is tax deductible.

Bibliography

BOOKS

American Personnel and Guidance Association (APGA). *Personnel and Guidance Standard Reference*. Washington, D.C.: APGA Press, 1973.

Blau, Peter. *The Dynamics of Bureaucracy*. 3d ed. Chicago: University of Chicago Press, 1963.

Carr-Saunders, A. M., and P. A. Wilson. *The Professions*. New York: Oxford University Press, 1933.

Davidson, Roger H. *The Politics of Comprehensive Manpower Legislation*. Baltimore: Johns Hopkins University Press, 1972.

Freidson, Eliot. *Profession of Medicine: A Study of the Sociology of Applied Knowledge*. New York: Dodd, Mead & Co., 1971.

Gerth, Hans, and C. Wright Mills (eds.). *From Max Weber: Essays in Sociology*. New York: Oxford University Press, 1946).

Levitan, Sar A., and Robert Taggart III. *Social Experimentation and Manpower Policy: The Rhetoric and the Reality*. Baltimore: Johns Hopkins University Press, 1971.

Lubove, Roy. *The Professional Altruist*. New York: Atheneum, 1973.

Matter, Joseph Allen. *Love, Altruism, and World Crisis: The Challenge of Pitirim Sorokin*. Chicago: Nelson-Hall Co., 1974.

Mirengoff, William, and Lester Rindler. *CETA: Manpower Programs under Local Control*. Staff paper prepared for the Committee on Evaluation of Employment and Training Programs. Washington, D.C.: National Academy of Sciences, 1978.

Parsons, Talcott (ed.). *Max Weber: The Theory of Social and Economic Organization*. New York: Free Press, 1964; originally published by Oxford University Press, 1947.

Perrow, Charles. *Organizational Analysis: A Sociological View*. Glenview, Ill.: Scott, Foresman and Co., 1972.

————. *Complex Organizations: A Critical Essay*. Glenview, Ill.: Scott, Foresman and Co., 1972.

Sorokin, Pitirim A. *Altruistic Love*. Boston: Beacon Press, 1950.

————. *The Ways and Power of Love*. Boston: Beacon Press, 1954.

Stanton, Esther. *Clients Come Last: Volunteers and Welfare Organizations*. Beverly
    Hills: Sage Publications, 1970.
Titmuss, Richard M. *The Gift Relationship: From Human Blood to Social Policy*. New
    York: Vintage Books, 1972.
Vidich, Arthur J., and Joseph Bensman. *Small Town in Mass Society*. Princeton,
    N.J.: Princeton University Press, 1968.
Weber, Max. "Bureaucracy." In *From Max Weber: Essays in Sociology*, eds. Hans
    Gerth and C. Wright Mills. New York: Oxford University Press, 1946.

ARTICLES

Goode, William J. "Community within a Community: The Professions." *Amer-
    ican Sociological Review*, April 1957.
Linder, Stephen H. "Administrative Accountability: Administrative Discretion,
    Accountability, and External Controls." In Scott Greer et al. (eds.), *Ac-
    countability in Urban Society: Public Agencies under Fire*. Beverly Hills: Sage
    Publications, 1978.
Lipsky, Michael. "The Assault on Human Services: Street-Level Bureaucrats,
    Accountability, and the Fiscal Crisis." In Scott Greer et al. (eds.), *Ac-
    countability in Urban Society: Public Agencies under Fire*. Beverly Hills: Sage
    Publications, 1978.
Obermann, C. Esco. "Report of the NRCA Ethics Subcommittee." *The Journal
    of Applied Rehabilitation Counseling*, Winter 1972–73.

GOVERNMENT DOCUMENTS

Statistical Abstract of the U.S. 1982–83. Washington, D.C.: Government Printing
    Office, 1983.
*An Assessment of CETA: Third Annual Report to the President and the Congress of
    the National Commission for Manpower Policy*. Special Report No. 7 of the
    National Commission for Manpower Policy. Washington, D.C.: Govern-
    ment Printing Office, May 1978.
CETA: An Analysis of the Issues. Special Report No. 23 of the National Commis-
    sion for Manpower Policy. Washington, D.C.: Government Printing Of-
    fice, May 1978.
Department of Labor Monitoring of Manpower Programs for the Hard to Employ.
    Hearings before a subcommittee of the Committee on Government Op-
    erations, House of Representatives, 95th Cong., 2d Sess. Washington,
    D.C.: Government Printing Office, 1979.
*Directions for a National Manpower Policy: A Collection of Policy Papers Prepared for
    Three Regional Conferences*. Washington, D.C.: Government Printing Of-
    fice, 1978.
The Implementation of CETA in Eastern Massachusetts and Boston. R & D Mono-
    graph 57. U.S. DOL, Employment and Training Administration. Wash-
    ington, D.C.: Government Printing Office, 1978.

Index

About the Author

JAMES LATIMORE is Assistant Professor in the Department of Sociology and Anthropology at the University of North Carolina at Charlotte. His articles have appeared in *Journal of Sociology and Social Welfare, The Bureaucrat, Public Productivity Review,* and other publications.